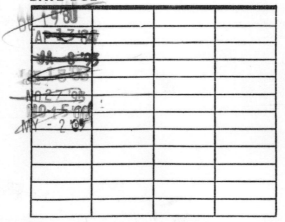

The Old Burial Ground, Charlestown, New Hampshire.

EARLY AMERICAN GRAVESTONE ART IN PHOTOGRAPHS

by
FRANCIS Y. DUVAL
and
IVAN B. RIGBY

DOVER PUBLICATIONS, INC.
NEW YORK

To the Memory of
MR. AXEL GROSSER
1912–1977

ACKNOWLEDGMENTS

The authors wish to express their sincere appreciation to the following individuals for their interest and assistance in local fieldwork:

Mr. and Mrs. S. G. Measamer, Circleville, Ohio; Mr. and Mrs. Robert A. Kolli, New Seabury, Massachusetts; Mr. James O. Joanou, Old Lyme, Connecticut; Mrs. Jessie Lie, South Hadley, Massachusetts; Messrs. Karl and Mackeath Stuecklen, Sandgate, Vermont; Mr. and Mrs. Deane Richardson, Worthington, Ohio; Mr. and Mrs. J. Richard Welch, Stonington, Maine; Mr. and Mrs. Robert Yingling, Plattsburgh, New York; Messrs. Albert E. Herbert and Roger Myers, Easthampton, Long Island, New York; Mr. and Mrs. James E. Rigby, Kingsport, Tennessee; Miss Katherine Rigby, Lancaster, Ohio; Mrs. Catherine Gibson, Madison, New Jersey; Mr. and Mrs. Jerry Trauber, Brooklyn, New York; Mr. and Mrs. A. S. Harvey, Jonesboro, Tennessee; Mr. Harold Dahlstrom, Essex, Connecticut; Mrs. Virginia Gizzi, Rehoboth, Massachusetts; Mr. and Mrs. Joseph B. Kapey, Syosset, Long Island, New York; Mrs. Elizabeth A. Masseli, Cromwell, Connecticut; Mr. and Mrs. Philip Jones, Moorestown, New Jersey; Mr. James B. Allen, South Hadley Falls, Massachusetts; Mr. and Mrs. Stewart Eidel, Old Lyme, Connecticut; Mr. Gene Buckingham, Delaware, Ohio; Mr. Warren H. Turner, Jr., Parish of Trinity Church, New York City; Rev. Raymond Wallace, First Presbyterian Church, Elizabeth, New Jersey.

Mention should also be made of the many anonymous residents of small communities in many parts of the country whose assistance was indispensable in locating remote burial grounds. Our most sincere gratitude.

F. Y. D.
I. B. R.

Published in Canada by General Publishing Company, Ltd., 30 Lesmill Road, Don Mills, Toronto, Ontario.

Published in the United Kingdom by Constable and Company, Ltd., 10 Orange Street, London WC2H 7EG.

Early American Gravestone Art in Photographs is a new work, first published by Dover Publications, Inc., New York, in 1978.

International Standard Book Number: 0–486–23689–7
Library of Congress Catalog Card Number: 78–54867

Manufactured in the United States of America
Dover Publications, Inc.
180 Varick Street
New York, N.Y. 10014

Contents

Foreword

Six years ago, when we took our first photographs of New England gravestones, we did not anticipate how intense our preoccupation with this fascinating art form would become. At this writing, we have travelled more than sixty thousand miles, from Maine to eastern Tennessee. We have crisscrossed most of the states in between and have visited nearly three thousand old burial grounds.

When we reach an old burial ground our procedure is as follows: we survey and annotate the enclosure and then photograph the grounds from various vantage points. We single out interesting gravestones and prepare them for black and white, and color photography. We brush these stones gently, wash them, carefully remove any lichen and weed around them. The gravestones are then systematically photographed in the field in full-view and in close-up.

Few communities restrict their old burial grounds. Some have posted signs, however, forbidding work of any kind, other than photography, within the enclosures. As our project evolved, we found it necessary to make molds of some gravestone carvings and we occasionally had to seek special permission for this process. We generally choose stones with unique styles or with particularly interesting symbols for the more complicated molding process with specially formulated compounds. The compounds must be applied and removed in the most exacting manner to avoid damaging the carvings in any way. It is a sophisticated process requiring skill and precise timing: it should not be imitated by amateurs. Since the stones must be meticulously cleaned before the compounds are applied and cleaned again when they are removed, the gravestones are always left in better condition than they are found.

In our studio, we attend to the molds: we remove the armatures, shore up the edges and then pour plaster into them. Each mold produces a three-dimensional replica with all the depth, detail and textural attributes of the original. When the mold is dry, we photograph each replica in the studio under lighting conditions far more flexible·than those at the stone's outdoor location. With such total control, the depth of execution and the refinement of carving may be emphasized and even dramatized, often giving the design unexpected qualities. Many of these replicas, photographed against black backgrounds, are included in this book.

We made all photographs with components of the Hasselblad system; a 500C/M single-lens reflex camera equipped with interchangeable lenses (80mm Planar f/2.8, 150mm Sonnar f/4, 250mm Sonnar f/5.6) and interchangeable magazines loaded with various film emulsions. We also took color transparencies in the course of the survey. When warranted, we used Proxar auxiliary close-up lenses and a Hasselblad Super Wide C with a Zeiss 38mm Biogon lens. We used Kodak Tri-X and Panatomic-X films in all field- and studio-work. They were exposed at the recommended ASA rating with a Gossen Lunasix light meter. The late Axel Grosser processed the film and Francis Y. Duval printed the negatives on an Omega D II enlarger, using Agfa-Gevaert Brovira papers (BN-111 #4, BH-111 #5, BEH-111 #6).

In this book are excerpts from our vast documentation. We hope it will increase an awareness of the cultural significance of this vanishing art legacy.

F. Y. D.
I. B. R.

Introduction

Fears about the uncertainty of an afterlife are rooted deeply in human nature, and nowhere are these anxieties better revealed than in grave markers immortalizing the spirit of the dead. Menhirs and obelisks, stelae and sarcophagi were all erected to symbolize the hereafter. The early Christians borrowed much of their eschatological imagery from more ancient faiths, but they eventually developed their own vocabulary which can be seen in the austere monuments of the Middle Ages and the ornate tombs of the Renaissance. During the Reformation, when the first religious immigrants fled Europe, they brought Christian imagery to these shores. The immigrants would foster the propagation of the memorial art form in seventeenth-century New England.

COLONIAL SETTLEMENTS

The influx of several thousand immigrants to the Massachusetts Bay Colony is documented in burial grounds by few grave markers predating the 1660s. This fact supports the belief that wood, not stone, marked the graves of the earliest settlers (painted and carved boards are known to have marked graves in seventeenth-century England). The natural impermanence of wood might explain the absence of markers from these first decades.

Notable among the few existing stone memorials from the earliest years are Ephraim Huit's in Windsor, Connecticut, dated 1644 (see p. 1), Richard Chester's in nearby Old Wethersfield, dated 1648 (see p. 1) and a fragment dated 1647 in the Old Burying Ground, laid out in 1634, in Ipswich, near the Massachusetts coast. Scores of pre-eighteenth-century slate gravestones can be seen in Massachusetts, while fine middle- and late-seventeenth-century sandstone specimens still stand in burial plots of neighboring states. Away from New England—on the southern coast, for instance—illegibility renders the true dating of even earlier markers virtually impossible.

There was never a need for stone imports in New England. The once-accepted theory of large-scale importing of memorials has been proved erroneous, at least in New England, where geological studies have confirmed the North American origin of the types of stone used. Several quarry sites were surveyed quite early and their exploitation decreed public. In Massachusetts, for example, there were slate quarries at Cambridge and Slate Island, near Quincy. Further north, schist was quarried at several locations in the Merrimack River basin. On the banks of the upper Connecticut River, Windsor settlers used the local red sandstone for a variety of purposes—including gravestones—as early as the mid-seventeenth-century. In later years, Portland brown sandstone and Norwich granite were quarried in great quantities at those inland locations and mica schist was quarried in other regions. Later still, white marble was discovered and exploited in such areas as southwest Vermont.

Stone slabs imported from abroad usually made the journey to the colonies as ballast and were used later for grindstones or in construction. There are no known shipping records of stones imported specifically for gravestone-making, but a few gravestones were probably ordered from abroad and erected on these shores. The Richard Churcher stone, dated 1681 (see p. 5), the oldest in Trinity Churchyard in New York City, is one such case. Both its front and back surfaces are carved and the stone is not a native type, so there is little doubt about its English origin. This example might indicate a trend in early New York of importing gravestones, a lack of local carving talent or quarry facilities, or perhaps an awareness or disapproval of the slate imagery then produced in the Massachusetts Bay Colony.

EARLY FUNERAL AND BURIAL RITES

In the earliest settlements, funeral rites were prescribed by Puritan factions from abroad. At these solemn rites, the congregation was forbidden to kneel, sing or recite prayers. They believed the fate of each soul was predetermined and that elaborate ceremony was of no avail. The only obsequies permitted were the tolling of a bell and a simple cortege to the gravesite. As the autonomy of local congregations grew, however, these rites were less and less adhered to. In some localities, funerals became more secular celebrations than sacred services. By the mid-eighteenth century, the secular aspects of the rites had so encroached upon the liturgical tradition that sumptuary laws were passed to curb excessive funeral displays.

By the turn of the eighteenth century, however, more solemn colonial customs had been established. A death in the community involved all the townspeople. Deaths were publicly posted. Prayers for the soul of the deceased were often requested and a death watch was organized for that purpose. When families could afford it, they sent silk gloves and rings as formal invitations to the funeral. Some families presented scarves of white linen to ministers, civil officials and prospective pallbearers. The house of the deceased was often draped in black and special hatchments were painted for the horses and the hearse. Lodging was made available to those journeying from afar and large amounts of food were prepared. A funeral sermon was written, printed and distributed while the deceased was afforded an uninterrupted vigil.

On the day of burial, a bell tolled and the pine coffin was carried by hearse to the meetinghouse or church for the official Christian rites, prayers and elegies. The bearers then shouldered the coffin while honorary pallbearers held symbolic palls over it. The black-clad congregation would then silently follow to the gravesite where a final elegy was intoned before burial.

BURIAL GROUNDS AND GRAVESTONES

Bereaved families soon began to erect stone markers as earthly remembrances for the deceased. The earliest stones lack carved designs and bear only minimal inscriptions: the initials of the deceased, his age and the year of death.[1] Later, the day and month of death and a touch of ornament were added. These generally crude slabs were common in the burial grounds of early settlements. In some areas, they remained in use until the 1730s. In time, the deceased came to be remembered by better-crafted vertical memorials, called headstones, symbolic portals to the life beyond.[2] Headstones were generally symmetrical with tympanum-topped center sections. They were inscribed at the center and flanked by borders. A smaller footstone was anchored parallel to the headstone some six feet away. Here, in a symbolic bed of repose, the deceased awaited the reward of resurrection.

In the mid-1670s, mortality-emblem carvings began to appear on headstones in the Massachusetts Bay Colony area: winged death's-heads, skeletons, skulls and crossbones, darts of death, coffins and bearers, palls and pallbearers, and gravediggers' implements. These stark images were at times juxtaposed with symbolic carvings of the passage of time, represented by the hourglass, the scythe, the candle and snuffer, and Father Time himself. Latin phrases were also used frequently, such as *Memento mori* (Remember that you must die), *Fugit hora* (The hour is fleeting) and *Memento te esse mortalem* (Remember that you are mortal). Such inscriptions and images were carved mainly in the immediate Massachusetts Bay Colony until the first decade of the eighteenth century. Similar images endured well beyond the 1780s in distant parts of the colonies, but these outmoded carvings would display fewer symbolic elements.

One should note here why such vivid imagery became common on early colonial gravestones. Meetinghouses and churches, because of their sacred function, were devoid of imagery. The secular life was not allowed to intrude on the sanctity of these buildings. But burial grounds were outside ecclesiastical jurisdiction; they were emphatically of this world. Even though gravestone carvings glorified the destiny of all men—death and the resurrection of the soul —they were aimed at the edification of the living. The colonists evidently enjoyed visiting their peaceful burial grounds and they were popular places for meditation. The carved designs, inscriptions and epitaphs undoubtedly gave the largely illiterate congregations a better understanding of Puritan moral precepts than did the ponderous sermons of the time.

The imagery of gravestone carvings was constantly evolving. The inventiveness of the carvers meant that richly carved new images were introduced alongside accepted ones. For example, coats of arms and escutcheon and hatchment carvings, indicative of lineage and wealth, appeared in Massachusetts around the 1690s. Their popularity spread in the coastal region; they remained in use, in Rhode Island especially, for over half a century on memorials of affluent families. The soul-effigy image also made its appearance in the latter part of the seventeenth century. This winged and sometimes crowned anthropomorphic representation of the soul and its ascent became more and more accepted over a period of several decades. Fostered by a less stringent orthodoxy, the soul-effigy was adapted to most regional styles and it is evident in all of New England's burial grounds. After the Revolutionary War, after nearly a century of acceptance, its popularity waned and it gave way to newer images, such as portraits, renditions of stations in life, trumpeters and celestial bodies.

TRADESMEN AND GRAVESTONE CARVERS

Early gravestone carvers were originally engaged in other stone-related work, such as masonry, bricklaying and roofing. In rural areas, braziers, surveyors and farmers joined their ranks. For most, gravestone carving started as an avocation. Early carvers bought or bartered stones from tradesmen who supplied them along with other building materials. Only a few carvers operated their own quarries. Some carvers always had enough slabs for gravestones and some even stocked cut memorials ready for inscription.

In rural areas, the bereaved usually had to be content with the local carver's style, but if he could afford it, he could buy a memorial by a carver from another region. Such a transaction was usually handled by a middleman who, for a fee, would take care of all correspondence and details. In population centers, a memorial could often be chosen from the works of several competing carvers.

The crude execution of many early markers indicates that stone engraving was not an easy task. Some carvers barely managed short inscriptions, but a few mastered the medium and produced primitive-looking yet forceful images adopted from funeral broadsides and sermons, emblem books, primers and woodcuts. But as more stone carvers began to devote their talents solely to the art form, they developed a visual language of their own and these influences became less important. Other colonial crafts, such as furniture-making and painting, smithing, weaving and embroidery, continued to exert a certain influence on gravestone styles, especially in the larger shipping centers.

To meet the demand for gravestones, a number of family workshops were established which created stylistically similar memorials over several years and, in some cases, over several generations. Entire Massachusetts families applied their talents to the art form during the seventeenth and eighteenth centuries: the Lamsons of Charlestown, the Emmeses of Boston, the Fosters of Dorchester, the Tingleys of Attleboro and the Parks of Harvard and Groton. A proud carving tradition was carried on simultaneously in the other colonies. For instance, while John Stevens II was learning the craft from his father in a Newport, Rhode Island shop, James Stanclift, Jr. was learning the trade from his father in a distant Connecticut quarry. Many carvers did not, of course, have talented family members to carry on their craft and relied on outside help in their shops. Many of these hired hands became quite proficient and some even surpassed their masters in skill and inspiration.

Most carvers practiced near their birthplaces. Only a few carvers, like John Hartshorn or Zerubbabel Collins, made distant moves during their careers. Few carvers managed to be at once inspired and successful during their lifetimes. Many left strong traditions but meager estates; many died forgotten, buried in unfit or unmarked graves.

THE PERIOD OF DECLINE

During the nineteenth century, the softening of religious attitudes led to a much less vigorous gravestone imagery. White marble memorials with cinerary-urn, willow and pilaster carvings became so widespread that burial grounds

---

[1]Before the adoption of the Gregorian calendar by England in 1752, many colonial carvers specified dates in both the Julian (Old Style) and Gregorian (New Style) calendar systems.

[2]Horizontal memorials were also fashioned from time to time: slabstones (flush with the ground), tombs (elevated from the ground with faced sides) and tablestones (slabstones elevated on supporting pillars). These memorials—most of them graceless —were executed primarily for ecclesiastical figures and the wealthy, and never gained wide acceptance.

of the period look antiseptic and monotonous. The large-scale adoption of Federal and Greek Revival motifs hastened the downfall of the art form. The coming of the industrial age made matters even worse. As monument companies were formed, gravestone art became even more impersonal and uninspired.

A few carvers did work in personal styles, however, and fine nineteenth-century examples may be encountered now and then. But these examples represent regional exceptions from the general rule of mediocrity. In Ohio, for instance, valuable gravestone images can be found in areas settled by Eastern colonists at the turn of the nineteenth century. The traditional carvers among these new settlers had not succumbed to the expediency of the times: their imagery and technique remained inspired and individual at a time when gravestone art was virtually devoid of symbolic significance and character. The appearance of such gravestone imagery outside New England is eloquent testimony to the endurance of the art form.[3]

But the paucity of valuable gravestone art becomes even more apparent from the 1880s on. Victorian burial grounds offer some interesting examples, but few talented artisans of the period showed any dedication to the art form. Most preferred to work on commissions from monument contractors. They supplied contractors with carved details for mausoleums and obelisks, large-scale memorials popular during the Victorian era. The triumph of technology in the twentieth century has further eclipsed the gravestone-carving tradition. The lack of inspired gravestone art today makes almost unbelievable the evidence that such a vibrant workshop-tradition once existed.

But the cultural legacy of centuries past remains in countless old burial grounds (a list of some of the more interesting and accessible ones can be found on p. 130). The inquisitive mind will find visiting them most rewarding, for their yards are open-air museums. Enter one and behold.

[3]A similar example can be traced to rural Pennsylvania. During the eighteenth century, in the eastern part of this region, traditionalist carvers adhered to the mid-European funeral imagery of its settlers. During the nineteenth century, these typical symbolic markers reappeared in isolated areas of southwest Virginia as a result of Lutheran congregations migrating from Pennsylvania.

The Old Durham Cemetery, Durham, Connecticut.

Top: Windsor, Connecticut, 1644. The Palisado Cemetery features the oldest legible date on any New England memorial. The following epitaph appears on the stone of the Rev. Ephraim Huit, "sometimes teacher to the church of Windsor": "who when hee lived, we drew our vitall breath, who when hee dyed, his dying was our death." Bottom: Old Wethersfield, Connecticut, 1648. This crude dragon-carving from the Chester coat of arms tops the tomb of Richard Chester, an armor bearer "Late of the Town of Blaby and Several other Lordships in Leistersheire."

ABOVE: Charlestown, Massachusetts, 1674. The austere image of mortality is prominent on Sara Long's slate in the Phipps Street Burial Ground. The small winged effigies on the border shoulders and the heart-shaped inscription area are unusual features for this early date. OPPOSITE TOP: Wakefield, Massachusetts, 1678. Capt. Jonathan Poole's stone displays the accepted gravestone symbolism of the early colonial period, as well as understated reminders of his rank in the British Army. OPPOSITE BOTTOM: Wakefield, Massachusetts, 1681. The Thomas Kendel slate displays unique imagery. As if victorious in death, the mortality emblem appears on a column surrounded by a winged hourglass, gravediggers' implements and Latin phrases about the earthly passage of time. Twin cherubim resting on a cloud-like frieze add to the visual impact.

ABOVE: Boston, Massachusetts, 1678. The Joseph Tapping slate stands at the entrance to the King's Chapel Burial Ground. Assembled on its surface are many of the Puritan symbols of death and the passage of time: the winged death's-head, the hourglass, the Latin phrases. The allegorical scene at the base continues the theme with the images of Father Time, death, the scythe and the symbolic snuffing of the candle of life. OPPOSITE TOP LEFT: Charlestown, Massachusetts, 1680. A different approach to death imagery is apparent on the many gravestones attributed to the still anonymous "Boston stonecutter." The small slate to the memory of Phinehas Pratt who "was on[e] of ye first English inhabitants of ye Massachusets Colony" is particularly well preserved. OPPOSITE TOP RIGHT: New York City, 1681. William Churcher apparently approved of the grim symbolism carved on the back of the gravestone of his five-year-old son Richard, which stands in Trinity Churchyard. Three factors suggest that the stone was executed in Britain and shipped to New York: the stone is not a native type; both the front and the back of the stone are carved; and the back carving itself is unusually deep. OPPOSITE BOTTOM: Marblehead, Massachusetts, 1683. The Mary Cromall slate on the old Burial Hill is a rarity among early gravestones. The winged death's-head is understated to the advantage of the strong border design and the prominent oblique sides.

6

SANCTORUM MEMORIA SIT BEATA

HERE LYETH BURIED
Yͤ BODY OF
Mͬ TIMOTHY LINDALL
AGED 56 YEARS
& 7 Mᵒ DECEASED
JANUARY Yͤ 6
1698 8/9

OPPOSITE TOP LEFT: Boston, Massachusetts, undated (probably 1690-1710). These numbered coats of arms were once part of tomb sidings. This example and several others are now free-standing near the entrance to the King's Chapel Burial Ground. OPPOSITE TOP RIGHT: Charlestown, Massachusetts, 1694. On the Timothy Cutler slate little imps are carrying a coffin. Both borders bear heads at the top and elaborate representations of gourds, which symbolized the passing of all earthly matters and the life to come. OPPOSITE BOTTOM: Scituate, Massachusetts, 1698. The style of this cutter was quite different from those of his contemporaries. He worked in the coastal area south of Boston and was probably a member of the Vinal family, for whom he carved several slate memorials. ABOVE: Salem, Massachusetts, 1698/9. The Timothy Lindall slate is one of the very few depicting death and the passage of time in border carvings. The central tympanum effigy is among the earliest in all New England.

ABOVE TOP LEFT: Milford, Connecticut, 1703. The carved initials of the deceased, "MC," appear with the side decorative elements on this roughly hewn footstone bearing a mortality emblem crowned by an hourglass. ABOVE TOP RIGHT: Quincy, Massachusetts, 1705. The large Joseph Penniman slate in the Hancock Cemetery also marks the grave of his twenty-year-old son Joseph. The area presumably reserved for his wife's inscription was never cut. ABOVE: Milford, Connecticut, 1698. The tympanum of Sarah Nisbett's slate displays Eros figures flanking a bowl

of fruit, symbolic of the plenitude of the afterlife. Like several others in the Boston area, this fine gravestone is marked "55" at its ground line, a "trademark" identified with an otherwise anonymous carver from the Massachusetts Bay Colony. OPPOSITE: Southampton, Long Island, New York, 1704. As status then demanded, the Howell coat of arms with its three castles was prominently displayed on Mathew Howell's gravestone. The inscription identifies him as "one of the House Representatives to Her Majesties Province of New York."

9

OPPOSITE: Wakefield, Massachusetts, 1709. One of the two identical, stylized likenesses of the Rev. Jonathan Pierpont reading his prayer book that appear on the shoulders of his gravestone, flanking the inscription area. ABOVE: Another detail from the Pierpont stone. This tympanum mortality motif shows a high degree of craftsmanship. It was carved by Joseph Lamson and his sixteen-year-old son Nathaniel, whose initials can be seen near the top border. Nathaniel customarily contributed to the execution, but the conception and date of the work suggest that the father was largely responsible for this stone, though he never signed any of his works.

Simsbury, Connecticut, 1710. The technique of the large mortality emblem
at the top of the Woodbridge tomb is crude, but an illusion of depth has
been achieved by the skull motif, which appears in an unusual perspective.

Newport, Rhode Island, 1724. John Stevens II carved this peacock, symbol of the incorruptibility of the flesh, as well as a coat of arms on commission from the Pelham family; they appear on a stone in the semiprivate Governor Arnold Burying Ground.

Here lies y Duſt of
Lievt John Hunt Deac
of y Church in Relio-
oth who departed thi
Life October y 23
1716. in y 62 Year
of his Age

The Saints which ſleep in Chriſt their head
are kept in Memory
When Chriſt who is our Life appears
They ſhall in Glory Riſe

OPPOSITE: Rumford, Rhode Island, 1716. This slate demonstrates the mastery of its cutter, George Allen, a Rehoboth sculptor whose signature appears at the lower left, half-hidden within the scroll, while the word "sculptor" appears at the lower right. This is an early appearance of the soul effigy on the tympanum (mortality emblems at this period being far more common). The Eros figures surrounding the heart-shaped inscription area would be unheard of for many years to come. ABOVE: Charlestown, Massachusetts, 1711. The stone of Capt. John Fowle, attributed to Joseph Lamson, is considered the most masterful of all the fine slates in the Phipps Street Burial Ground. A large coat of arms forms its central motif. It is topped by a soul effigy on the tympanum, while the small inscription area has been relegated to a position near the ground line.

15

Above: Rowley, Massachusetts, 1717. This distinctive design style has been traced to John Hartshorne, a Haverhill-area cutter whose work is widely distributed throughout Essex County. Further examples of his gravestone carvings are found in eastern Connecticut, an area he moved to and continued to practice in from the 1720s on. **Opposite top:** Newbury, Massachusetts, 1728. This unusually well preserved gravestone is from the coastal region north of Boston, where schist was quarried in great quantity; it is the work of Robert Mulican, a nearby Bradford carver. **Opposite bottom:** Elizabeth, New Jersey, 1727. An early Elizabethtown artisan produced this striking carving. The death's-head and the hourglass were traditional symbols for mortality and the passage of time. The doves symbolize the soul. Such a juxtaposition of images was seldom attempted on New England memorials.

Here lies Inter'd the
Body of James, ÿ Son
of John & Lydia Procter
Deceased Febuary ÿ 3.d
1729. Aged 16 Months

Save Fruitless Tears & Weep no more
This Child's not left But gone before.
Deaths a Haven towards ÿ all Winds drive
And where ÿ shall each Mortal spirit arive:
Be therefore Wife ÿ when thy Corps shall lye
At Anchor thus, thy Soul may mount on High

OPPOSITE TOP LEFT: Providence, Rhode Island, 1729. John Stevens II departed from the Harris family's traditional three-bird crest motif by placing the birds in symbolic vines. This is the Job Harris slate, one of the last commissioned by the family. OPPOSITE TOP RIGHT: New London, Connecticut, 1729. This stone was imported from the Rhode Island Colony by the Procter family in memory of their infant son. Unlike others in the Ancient Burying Ground, this fine slate has only slightly weathered over the years. OPPOSITE BOTTOM: Elizabeth, New Jersey, 1733. The tympanum of the Robert Ogden brownstone offers a rare soul effigy with downward, overlapping wings, a stylistic approach rarely ventured on New England gravestones. ABOVE: Haverhill, Massachusetts, ca. 1735. A rare and sinister winged death's-head by an anonymous coastal stone-cutter.

ABOVE: Middletown, Connecticut, 1742. This unusual carving marks a transition from death's-head to soul effigy; it bears attributes of both. OPPOSITE TOP LEFT: Whippany, New Jersey, 1733. The cutter of this early eighteenth-century brownstone from the lower Hudson region sacrificed the usual border designs to accommodate the larger shield-shaped inscription area. OPPOSITE TOP RIGHT: Essex, Connecticut, 1735. This diminutive brownstone of a rare style is from the lower Connecticut River valley. Its origin is probably further upstream, where this style with the effigy overlapping the inscription area, is sometimes encountered. OPPOSITE BOTTOM: Haverhill, Massachusetts, 1735. The tympanum of this schist gravestone displays typical imagery carved by Robert Mulican during the first half of the eighteenth century.

OPPOSITE TOP LEFT: Columbia, Connecticut, ca. 1740. Benjamin Collins is credited with this style of carving; it was executed on coarse granite, which may account for its strong linear quality. OPPOSITE TOP RIGHT: Boston, Massachusetts, 1747. This distinctive mortality emblem marks the grave of John Grover in the King's Chapel Burial Ground. OPPOSITE BOTTOM: Plymouth, Massachusetts, 1745. The emblems of the pilgrimage of life (the shell), time and death as they appear on Thomas Faunce's slate on the historic Burial Hill. ABOVE: Lancaster, Massachusetts, 1747. The slate to the memory of Dr. John Dunsmoor and his three children stands in the Old Settlers' Burial Field. Two angels representing souls in bliss flank the main heart motif, which is repeated for each of the three children.

24

OPPOSITE TOP: Providence, Rhode Island, 1745. The Harris coat of arms adorns Mrs. Doreas Smith's headstone. She married a member of the Harris family, which traditionally used a three-bird motif on family memorials. OPPOSITE BOTTOM: Union, Connecticut, 1745/6. The tympanum of Ebenezer Waman's gravestone features one of New England's most striking soul effigies, in the later style of Obadiah Wheeler. Wheeler was a Lebanon artisan whose work is widely distributed in eastern Connecticut. ABOVE: Lancaster, Massachusetts, 1747/8. Jonathan Worcester, a Harvard carver, evolved this skull design; it is prominently displayed on the tympanum of all his gravestone commissions executed before the middle of the eighteenth century.

26

OPPOSITE TOP: Durham, Connecticut, 1748. A solitary crown, symbol of the reward of the righteousness, was a popular eighteenth-century footstone motif, but it rarely appeared on headstones, as it does here. OPPOSITE BOTTOM: Middletown, Connecticut, 1747/8. The effigy carved at the top of Capt. Samuel Willis's brownstone in the remote Riverside Cemetery is exceptional because it is not symmetrical. ABOVE: New York City, 1749. This stark soul effigy on an unadorned pediment and a crude inscription mark the severe gravestone of Andrew Mills, "Purser of his Majestys Ship Greyhound" in Trinity Churchyard.

OPPOSITE TOP: Woodstock, Connecticut, 1752. On this slate stone is one of only two clock carvings, indicating the symbolic hour of death, known to appear on gravestones. This image replaced the hourglass usually associated with the passage of time. The stone's design retains the twin mortality emblems of the gravedigger's tools and the crossbones. OPPOSITE BOTTOM: Barnstable, Massachusetts, 1741. Found in the Cape Cod area, this motif is typical of Nathaniel Fuller's later approach to gravestone symbolism; it probably symbolized the release of the deceased's spirit. ABOVE: Felchville, Vermont, 1754. This rendition appears atop one of two slates jointly protected in a granite casing. It commemorates an Indian kidnapping of early settlers during which "Mrs. Johnson was Delivrd of her Child Half a mile up this Brook." The newborn died during the incident, and an adjacent marker is to the child's memory. (See detail on page 30.)

OPPOSITE TOP: Felchville, Vermont, 1754. This is the crude carving at the ground line of the small slate memorial to the Johnson infant. OPPOSITE BOTTOM: Long-meadow, Massachusetts, 1757. Flanked by Scottish thistles, the lone hourglass on Mary Bliss's brownstone memorial forcefully symbolizes the termination of her earthly life. Aaron Bliss, probably a relation, is credited with its concept and execution. ABOVE: Newport, Rhode Island, 1751. A striking soul effigy in a style popular in the middle of the eighteenth century. Though this approach is frequently encountered throughout southern New England, its originator has never been identified.

In Memory of ye three
Children of Mr Samuel

OPPOSITE TOP: Milton, Massachusetts, 1760. A rather late manifestation of mortality and time imagery tops Lt. Robert Vose's slate; the once-popular motifs appear here in a scattered but nevertheless effective arrangement. OPPOSITE BOTTOM: Longmeadow, Massachusetts, 1760. The striking and rare imagery on the Naomi Woolworth brownstone presents death, time and repentance motifs on its tympanum. ABOVE: Norwichtown, Connecticut, 1759. The three Manning children appear as bat-like effigies on their joint memorial. This granite carving is attributed to stonemason Samuel Manning, the father of the children.

ABOVE: Lexington, Massachusetts, ca. 1760. Executed in a carving style found frequently in the Old Burying Ground near Lexington's famous Green, this rendition, by virtue of the winged frame, qualifies more as a soul effigy than a portrait. OPPOSITE TOP LEFT: Bristol, Rhode Island, 1759. Colonial families often had their coats of arms carved on their memorials. One of the better-preserved stones is the Joseph Reynolds slate in the East Burial Ground. OPPOSITE TOP RIGHT: Enfield, Connecti-

cut, 1763. The architectural features of Capt. Samuel Dwight's marker strongly suggest the entrance to eternity through the portal of death. OPPOSITE BOTTOM: Rutland, Massachusetts, 1760. William Young is credited with this carving style and approach to symbolism. The figure would be considered wingless were it not for the presence of birds at its shoulders, symbolizing the flight of the soul and a variant of the then-traditional soul effigy.

In Memory of Eld^r
George Clarke He Died
Augt as y^e 21 AD 1762
Aged 82 Years
Blessed Are y^e Dead
That Dⁱln y^e lord

OPPOSITE: Durham, Connecticut, 1760. On Capt. Nathanael Sutlief's gravestone the crown of Christian righteousness stands above the crossed swords representing his military profession. Twin mortality emblems accompany the inspirational epitaph of this massive brownstone in the Old Durham Cemetery. ABOVE: Seymour, Connecticut, 1762. A surprising find in a little-known cemetery, this stone probably shows some amateur's attempt at gravestone making for a loved one. Its style is unique and it is carved from common field stone. It is a true homemade commodity, simply executed but quite inventive.

ABOVE: Northborough, Massachusetts, 1764. Rabbi Judah Monis was Hebrew instructor at Harvard College. His inscription records that he was converted and "publickly baptizd" at Cambridge in 1722. William Park carved his slate with this deep skull-and-crossbones motif at the center. OPPOSITE TOP: East Glastonbury, Connecticut, 1762. Peter Buckland, an East Hartford carver, signed the Deacon Daniel House brownstone. Surrounding the effigy are the images of the sacramental vines (the body of Christ) and hearts (the love of Christ). OPPOSITE BOTTOM: Hadley, Massachusetts, 1765. This unusual crowned effigy is highlighted by deep carving. Inward-pointing wings and distinctive eyelids were some of the features preferred by the anonymous rural artisan who executed many of these figures in local brownstone.

TOP: Woodstock, Connecticut, 1764. The greenish Jamina McClallan slate presents a winged effigy with this rare spider-like quality, few examples of which are to be found in all New England. BOTTOM LEFT: Peterborough, New Hampshire, 1765. The Samuel and Hannah Todd stone is attributed to a Londonderry carver named John Wight.

Wight's strong hieroglyphic style is widely distributed in southern New Hampshire. BOTTOM RIGHT: Hollis, New Hampshire, ca. 1765. The right tympanum effigy carving on the Emerson children's memorial; Abel Webster is credited with its execution. Several other slates by this local artisan are in the Center Burying Ground.

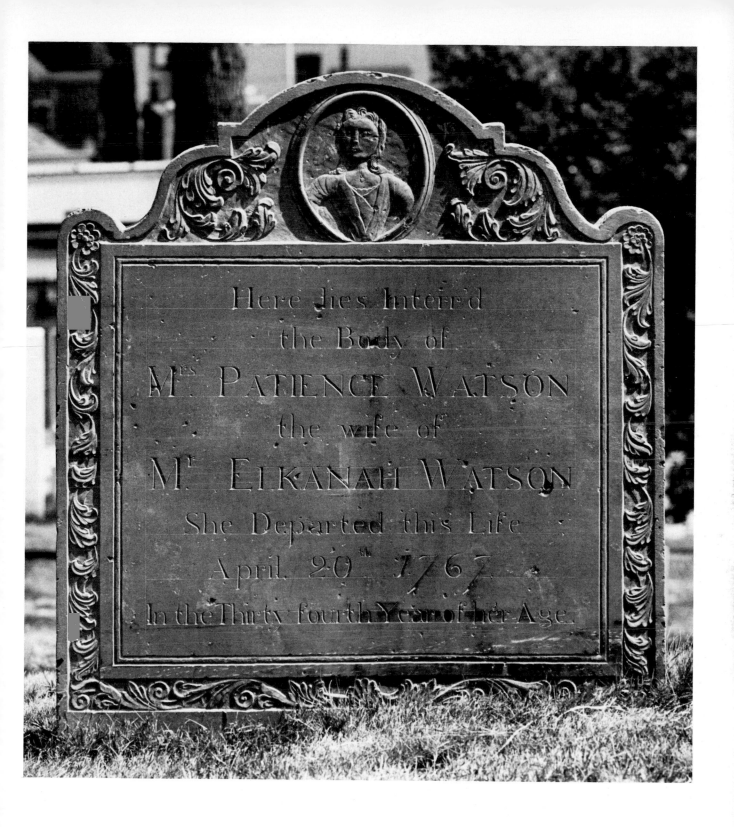

Here lies Interr'd
the Body of
Mrs PATIENCE WATSON
the wife of
Mr ELKANAH WATSON
She Departed this Life
April 20th 1767
In the Thirty fourth Year of her Age.

ABOVE: Plymouth, Massachusetts, 1767. William Codner, a Boston carver, became fashionable for his fine slate portraits. Patience Watson's memorial rates among the finest ones executed in the latter part of his successful career.

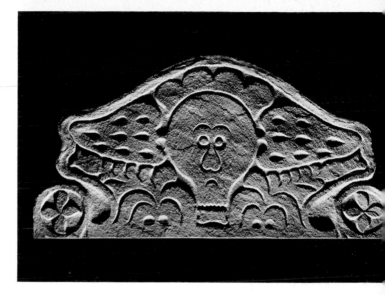

OPPOSITE TOP: Chelmsford, Massachusetts, 1767. The tympanum of Elizabeth Clark's slate bears this extraordinary carving of a trumpeting figure heralding the resurrection. OPPOSITE BOTTOM: Bristol, Rhode Island, 1767. Sara Swan's slate bears this unique allegory reflecting on the inscription from 1 Corinthians 15:22: "For as in Adam all die, even so in Christ shall all be made alive." LEFT: Braintree, Massachusetts, 1768. Lt. Nathaniel Thayer's gravestone has border carvings symbolizing the just rising at the trumpet call for the resurrection. The left border is the better preserved; it is pictured here with its underground area exposed for the first time. ABOVE TOP: New York City, 1766. This style of soul effigy is native to early New York. Only two examples remain, both in the Trinity Churchyard. ABOVE BOTTOM: Farmington, Connecticut, 1766. These humorous effigies are found in many areas of New England. Gershom Bartlett is recognized as the originator of this style, but many local stonecutters are suspected of imitating his work.

RIGHT: Newport, Rhode Island, 1769. Capt. Nathaniel
Waldron's slate is one of the most ambitious carvings by
young John Stevens, Jr. This detail, one of two exotic
border figures holding flowering standards, appears to the
left of the inscription area. OPPOSITE TOP: Northampton,
Massachusetts, 1769. Capt. John Lyman's stone bears
this intensely mystical imagery of the partaking of the
sacramental vines. OPPOSITE BOTTOM: Williamstown,
Massachusetts, 1771. The Elisabeth Smith marble, among
the earliest of its type, offers one of New England's most
primitive-looking carvings.

IN MEMORY of
SARAH Wife of
WILLIAM BENTLY

EDWARD SCOTT
Junr Whose Body

OPPOSITE: Rumford, Rhode Island, 1770. Coat-of-arms detail atop Jabez Bowen's tomb in the Newman Cemetery. This imagery indicated Bowen's status in the community as a physician and surgeon at a time when such carvings were no longer popular. ABOVE: Newport, Rhode Island, 1767. The Sarah Bently slate is attributed to John Bull, who executed only a few of these sorrowful effigies surrounded by the scythe and the hourglass. LEFT: Newport, Rhode Island, ca. 1765. The Common Burying Ground offers a few variants of these plump looking cherub designs. Nearly all are juxtaposed with one or more mortality emblems.

In Memory of Capt Hezekiah
Stone Who Departed this Life
July ye 18th 1771 in the
61st year of his Age.

Benath this Stone Deaths Primer lies
the Stone Shall moue the Primer Rife

OPPOSITE: Ephrata, Pennsylvania, 1770. This unusually massive sandstone memorial stands in the Bergstrasse Lutheran Churchyard. Both sides bear tightly carved inscriptions, and the lower front area displays mortality emblems in high relief. ABOVE: Oxford, Massachusetts, 1771. Capt. Hezekiah Stone's memorial features one of the bright-eyed effigies attributed to the Soule family, which is known to have produced several stonecutters.

OPPOSITE TOP: Milton, Massachusetts, 1771. The Seth Sumner slate is the only specimen signed by its carver, Henry Christian Geyer. The tympanum bears a vision of heavenly glory. OPPOSITE BOTTOM LEFT: Pomfret, Connecticut, 1771. The large rectilinear slate for Mr. and Mrs. Nathaniel Sessions is signed by sculptor George Allen. It displays a large inscription area flanked by twin effigies at its upper corners; only the left carving (shown here) remains undamaged. OPPOSITE BOTTOM RIGHT: Newport, Rhode Island, 1772. Pompey Brenton was one of the many African slaves to be buried in the Common Burying Ground. His slate is signed by John Stevens, Jr. ABOVE: Newport, Rhode Island, 1773. The only known carving of God on a New England gravestone can be seen on the tympanum of Charles Bardin's memorial. The large slate is initialled "J.B."—John Bull, Newport's famous carver.

ABOVE: Spencer, Massachusetts, 1776. Jonathan Snow's gravestone displays this deep portrait-like carving with a distinctive Indian hair style. OPPOSITE TOP: New York City, 1772. This very beautiful memorial in the Trinity Churchyard is the work of an anonymous artist. The upper part features this portrait of infant Margaret Barron, framed at its corners by flanking cherubs. OPPOSITE BOTTOM: Norwichtown, Connecticut, ca. 1775. This well-preserved example is probably from the Lamb family workshop. Most specimens of this compact style are rapidly shaling due to the unstable nature of the stone on which they were rendered.

ABOVE: Marblehead, Massachusetts, 1776. The Susanna Jayne slate is attributed to Henry Christian Geyer, and its central motif attests to his creativity. Symbols of time, mortality and the resurrection are framed within the hooped snake of eternity. The angels in the upper corners and the bats in the lower signify the supremacy of good over evil. OPPOSITE TOP LEFT: New York City, ca. 1775. The date has disappeared on this rare double-effigy brown-stone, one of the least-eroded in the St. Paul's Chapel Burial Ground. OPPOSITE TOP RIGHT: Newburyport, Massachusetts, 1776. Though he was 80 when he died, Capt. Anthony Gwyn is pictured on his slate as a young and dashing officer. OPPOSITE BOTTOM: Falmouth, Massachusetts, 1776. This eroded example from the Old Town Burying Ground presents an effigy in profile, a rarity in gravestone imagery.

54

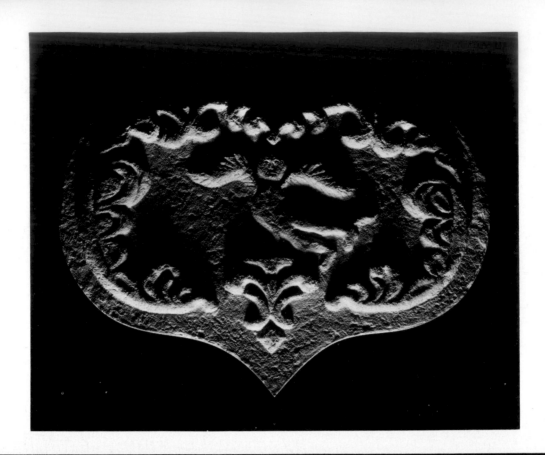

OPPOSITE TOP: Brickerville, Pennsylvania, 1777. The two-sided sandstone memorial of James Old, who died at the age of four, displays this small effigy. OPPOSITE BOTTOM: Northampton, Massachusetts, 1777. "CSP" are the initials of Colonel Seth Pomroy; on this tympanum by stonecutter Nathaniel Phelps, symbols of Pomroy's military career surround heralds of the resurrection. ABOVE: Cheshire, Connecticut, 1777. The Reverend and Mrs. Samuel Hall died within a year of each other and are thus portrayed jointly in this remarkable carving.

ABOVE: Boston, Massachusetts, 1780. Lt. Jabez Smith's gravestone in Boston's historic Granary Burying Ground is as much a memorial to the Continental ship *Trumbull* as it is a personal one. The twenty-nine-year-old Smith died on board ship during an encounter with the British fleet off Bermuda. The ship which was captured by the British, dismantled and used as firewood, is here remembered as "Anchor'd in the haven of Rest." OPPOSITE TOP LEFT: Huntington, Long Island, New York, 1778. The memorial of the Conkling children displays overlapping twin effigies. All slate gravestones on Long Island orig-

inated on the mainland. This example was probably shipped from the Rhode Island Colony. OPPOSITE TOP RIGHT: Muddy Creek, Pennsylvania, ca. 1785. This high-relief portrait atop a memorial carved on two sides probably dates from the 1780s. Like many Pennsylvania German gravestones of this period, it bears no inscription. OPPOSITE BOTTOM: Northampton, Massachusetts, 1780. This unique carving, attributed to Nathaniel Phelps, attempts a symbolic juxtaposition of death and the resurrection.

59

Charles Brigham

OPPOSITE: Muddy Creek, Pennsylvania, undated. Many German memorials offer striking but obscure imagery. This is one of the most interesting of these uninscribed brownstones from the latter part of the eighteenth cen-tury. ABOVE: Grafton, Massachusetts, 1781. Magistrate Charles Brigham is portrayed as young and fit as he passes through the portal of eternity on his gravestone tympanum.

61

OPPOSITE TOP LEFT: Farmington, Connecticut, 1782. William Hooker's brownstone displays this simple medallion showing the bud of renewed life sprouting from the grave. OPPOSITE TOP RIGHT: Brooklyn, Connecticut, 1782. Capt. Benjamin Peirce, his three wives and his only child are all portrayed on the family memorial. OPPOSITE BOTTOM: South Hadley, Massachusetts, 1783. Profiles of his two wives flank the full-face portrait of the Rev. John Woodbridge on this joint brownstone memorial. ABOVE: Chelmsford, Massachusetts, 1783. This rare example of a mortality emblem from the latter part of the eighteenth century is on Sarah Bridge's slate. Though outdated at the time of its creation, this image remains one of the most forceful ever carved in New England.

ABOVE: Bristol, Rhode Island, 1785. The handsome Juniper Hill Cemetery offers only one notable slate memorial, that of Dr. Thomas Munro, which portrays the physician in an appropriate healing gesture. OPPOSITE TOP: Hampton, Connecticut, 1785. Lucy Fuller's gravestone tympanum displays the Federal eagle, an adaptation of the new nation's emblem to gravestone imagery. This carving is attributed to Lebbeus Kimball, one of a family of eastern Connecticut carvers. OPPOSITE BOTTOM: Southampton, Long Island, New York, ca. 1785. This carving style is characteristic of the Zuricher workshop, which was located in or near New York City. John Zuricher himself occasionally signed some of its output, which invariably presented round-cheeked effigies like this one.

ABOVE: Montowese, Connecticut, 1786. This brownstone portrait of a haughty lady prefigures the more stylized portraiture prevalent in central Connecticut in the late 1790s. OPPOSITE TOP LEFT: Newport, Rhode Island, 1786. Bicentennial refurbishing unearthed the underground portion of the Tripp children's slate and revealed a test carving of Mrs. Tripp's amputated arm. The arm was buried in the children's plot, and the final carving was cut at the slate's center. OPPOSITE TOP RIGHT: Delta, Pennsylvania, 1790. A totally different carving style and configuration characterize a few Pennsylvania sandstone memorials. Mortality emblems which at this time were already outdated in New England were still in vogue in rural Pennsylvania. OPPOSITE BOTTOM: New York City, 1787. Three fieldpieces appear at the top of Daniel Rowls Carpenter's gravestone in Trinity Churchyard. Its eroded inscription records that "he was a member of the Company of Officers sent to this place by the Honorable Boared of Ordinance under the direction of Major Dixon: Chief engineer of America."

ABOVE: Auburn, Massachusetts, 1786. Attributed to James New, this fine slate portrait shows seven-year-old Peter Bancroft as a well-groomed young gentleman. OPPOSITE TOP: Newport, Rhode Island, 1786. The Langley children's memorial consists of six small effigies on a nine-foot-wide slate slab. John Bull signed the stone, one of the many stunning gravestones in the immense Common Burying Ground. OPPOSITE BOTTOM: Lower Saucon Township, Pennsylvania, 1787. The Christ Church Burial Ground offers a few of these interesting gravestone carvings. Executed in coarse sandstone, the imagery usually includes an effigy flanked by birds—in this case roosters, probably symbolic of repentance.

Here lie Deposited Six Children Sons and daughters of Mr WILLIAM LANGLEY and SARAH his Wife.
SARAH died Feb Alfo NATHANIEL Alfo SARAH the 2d Alfo ROYAL Alfo SARAH the 3d Alfo WILLIAM

Here lie Six bleised Babes which JESUS said His bleised Kingdom should be made.
Then every Mourning Heart chear up with this that with their Saviour art in endlefs blifs.

cutt by J.Bull

OPPOSITE TOP: East Bridgewater, Massachusetts, 1787. The Rev. John Angier is portrayed in the pulpit on the tympanum of his slate memorial in The Old Grave Yard. OPPOSITE BOTTOM: Charlestown, Massachusetts, 1787. Polly Harris's slate adapts outdated Puritan imagery, in which a death brandishes his dart at the image of the deceased. ABOVE: Ephrata, Pennsylvania, undated. Probably from the 1790s, this winged effigy appears on the front of a memorial that is carved on two sides. Its high relief was executed on a massive slab of textured sandstone which bears no identification whatsoever.

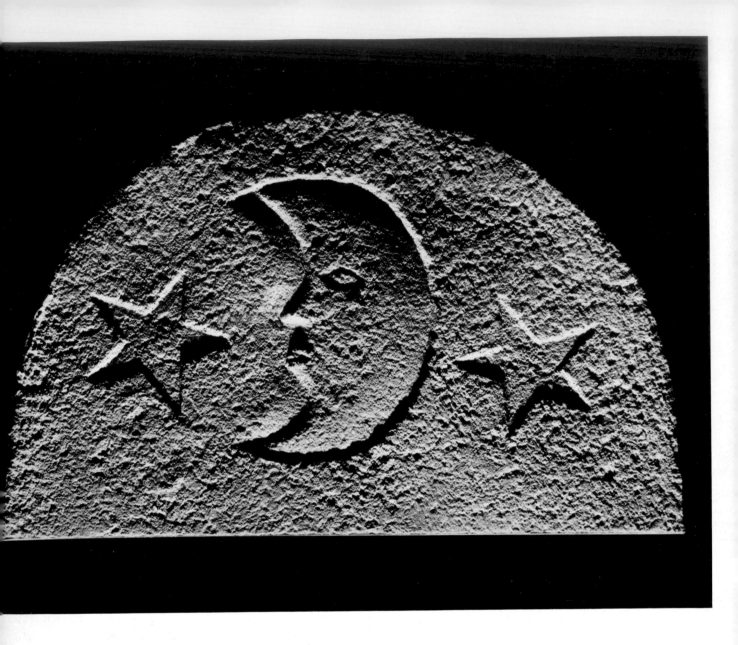

ABOVE: Bowmansville, Pennsylvania, undated. Like most of the similar carvings found here, this one is without inscription or date. The moon and stars probably represent the time cycles of earthly existence. The stone probably dates from the late eighteenth century. OPPOSITE TOP: Durham, Connecticut, 1789. This style of crowned effigy is common in the many Connecticut River valley burial grounds. They were carved out of an unstable Portland brownstone which tends to split and crumble. This exam-ple has so far escaped serious damage by erosion. OPPO-SITE BOTTOM LEFT: Bennington, Vermont, 1790. This twin effigy marble memorial for the Swift infant daughters is in the Old Bennington Cemetery. The typical southern Vermont gravestone configuration has been adapted for this unusual function. OPPOSITE BOTTOM RIGHT: Bricker-ville, Pennsylvania, 1791. A few burial grounds in Lan-caster County abound with stones in this ornate style, carved in coarse sandstone.

ABOVE: Wendell, Massachusetts, 1790. The Kilburn youngsters are remembered by this unique carving in a remote burial yard of western Massachusetts. OPPOSITE: New Salem, Massachusetts, 1790. The glorified soul appears thus in a number of highly original gravestone carvings in north-central Massachusetts. Carved in rough local stone types, these images are among the most inventive in all New England.

ABOVE: Sutton, Massachusetts, 1792. Flanked by heavenly symbols, a cherub heralding the resurrection points to the message, "As we rise, sing glory glory, through the skies." RIGHT: Shaftsbury Center, Vermont, 1794. Amy Clark's marble memorial shows a soul effigy in a floral setting underneath a mortality inscription. This style is attributed to Zerubbabel Collins, a Connecticut carver who moved to southern Vermont late in his career.

TOP: Barnstable, Massachusetts, 1790. A small herald proclaims the advent of the resurrection on this slate in the Lothrop Cemetery. BOTTOM: Belchertown, Massachusetts, 1792. The upper part of Hannah Dwight's slate displays a stylized portrait surrounded by floral and geometric designs. The memorial is initialed "E.S." for one of the Sikes family of carvers, whose output is well represented in many New England burial grounds.

In Memory of

Mrs. ANNA

HITCHCOCK 2d

Confort to Mr.

Amasa Hitchcoc k

who died Oct. 6th

AD. 1795 Æ. 27.

In Memory
of Amasa
B. Hitchco ck
fon to Mr.
Amasa
& Mrs.
ANNA
Hitchcoc k
who died
Sept. 3d.
AD. 1795
Æ. 3 years.

In Memory
of two
of their
Children
who died
in Infancy.

Ye young ye fair your rofed cheek

May promife you old age

But yet a few more fetting funs

memento mori

IN MEMORY OF

Mr Walker Stillfon, who
Died August the 8th A

OPPOSITE: Cheshire, Connecticut, 1795. This deeply carved masterpiece in the Hillside Cemetery has an ornate setting for the evocative portrait of Mrs. Anna Hitchcock, mother of the children profiled on the shoulders. ABOVE: Sandgate, Vermont, 1796. This whimsical style is widely encountered in southwestern Vermont. These exquisite marble carvings are attributed to Samuel Dwight, a local sculptor whose signature is found on some of them.

This Monument is erected to the Memory of Four Lovely
and promiſing Sons of Mr. Appleton & Mrs. Lydia Holmes.

Appleton died Feb. 24th D 179[?] | Burridg died Dec. 10th D 1794
in the 9th Year of his Age~ | in the 12th Year of his Age~
Ozias died Feb. 2[?]d D 179[?] | Calvin died Feb. 25th D 1793
in the 7th Year of his Age. | in the 12th Year of his Age~

No living mortal ſee in coſtly Bloom,
Four lovely offsprings lie beneath this tomb.
The afflicted mother weeps from day to day,
To ſee theſe lovely branches torn away~
But whilſt you weep the Lamb on Calvery ſlain,
Feeds the young Branches which ſhall ſprout again.
Whilſt God the FARTHER who all heaven ſupplies,
Shall wipe the ſorrows from the parents eyes~

ABOVE: East Glastonbury, Connecticut, 1795. This superb brownstone "to the Memory of Four Lovely and promising Sons of Mr. Appleton & Mrs. Lydia Holmes" is the work of an unknown carver. On the right, twins Burridge and Calvin face each other, separated from their younger brothers, Appleton and Ozias, by a symbolic tree of life with four severed branches. OPPOSITE TOP LEFT: Arlington, Vermont, 1796. This strongly linear portrait to the memory of Miriam Hawley was probably conceived and executed by Samuel Dwight, a Shaftsbury carver. OPPOSITE TOP RIGHT: Charlestown, New Hampshire, 1796. The prominent wings on these lightly carved effigies are in a style once popular in southern Vermont and New Hampshire. OPPOSITE BOTTOM: Columbia, Connecticut, 1797. The tympanum of Deacon Israel Woodward's granite memorial displays this austerely beautiful soul effigy.

ABOVE: Charlestown, New Hampshire, 1797. The Willard family memorial portrays the father and mother in addition to a seated winged figure; the flowering buds probably refer to their children. The inscription begins, "Erected in Memory of Lieut. Moses Willard and Mrs. Susannah, his Wife Who Were first Settlers of this Town; Whose boddys are inter'd here. He was Killd by the Indians June 16th 1756 In the 54th year of his age And she departed this Life May 5th 1797 In the 88th year of her age." The inscription goes on to point out that "What render'd their lives remarkable was that their being bereft of two of their elder daughters by the Indians; one of whom had her family with her and continued in captivity till after his death." OPPOSITE: Essex, Connecticut, 1797. Under the ever-watchful eyes of God, a unique juxtaposition of the New and Old Testaments is displayed on the Eliakim Hayden gravestone. The cross of redemption and the soul, symbolized by the dove, top the ark of salvation and echo the epitaph: "As in Adam, all mankinde, Did guilt and Death Derive, So by the Righteousness of Christ, Shall all be made alive."

Sacred to the Memory of

Cap.ⁿ Moſes Porter.	Mrs. Elizabeth.
who was born at	Relict of Capt.
Hadley January	Moses Porter.
13.ᵈ A.D. 1721. & was	who was born
ſlain by the Indians	at Eaſt Hartford
near Crown Point	Oc.ᵗ 4.ᵗ A.D. 1719.
in the Morning ſcout	and died at
of the 8.ᵗʰ of Sep.ʳ	Hadley Oc.ᵗ 2.ᵈ
1755.	1798.

Earth's evry ſtation ends in "Here he lies"
But Life immotal waits beyond the Grave.

In Memory of
Mrs. Submit wife of
Simeon Chittenden Esq.

OPPOSITE: Hadley, Massachusetts, 1798. The serenity of the portraits of Moses and Elizabeth Porter atop their large marble memorial suggests the reward of righteous- ness. ABOVE: North Guilford, Connecticut, 1796. Mrs. Sub- mit Chittenden's stone bears her profile in a style typical of local efforts at portraiture.

ABOVE: Meriden, Connecticut, 1797. The medallion on Lucretia Hough's brownstone features a stylized portrait by an innovative artisan from southern Connecticut. OPPOSITE TOP: Warrenville, New Jersey, 1798. Twin symbols of the soul appear on the tympanum of Phebe Davison's brownstone in the Mount Bethel Baptist Meeting House yard. Its cutter, Jonathan Hand Osborn, signed it prominently. OPPOSITE BOTTOM: West Suffield, Connecticut, 1799. This bold style of crowned effigy is plentiful in some burial grounds of the upper Connecticut River valley. They were carved in redstone, which has proved impervious to natural erosion.

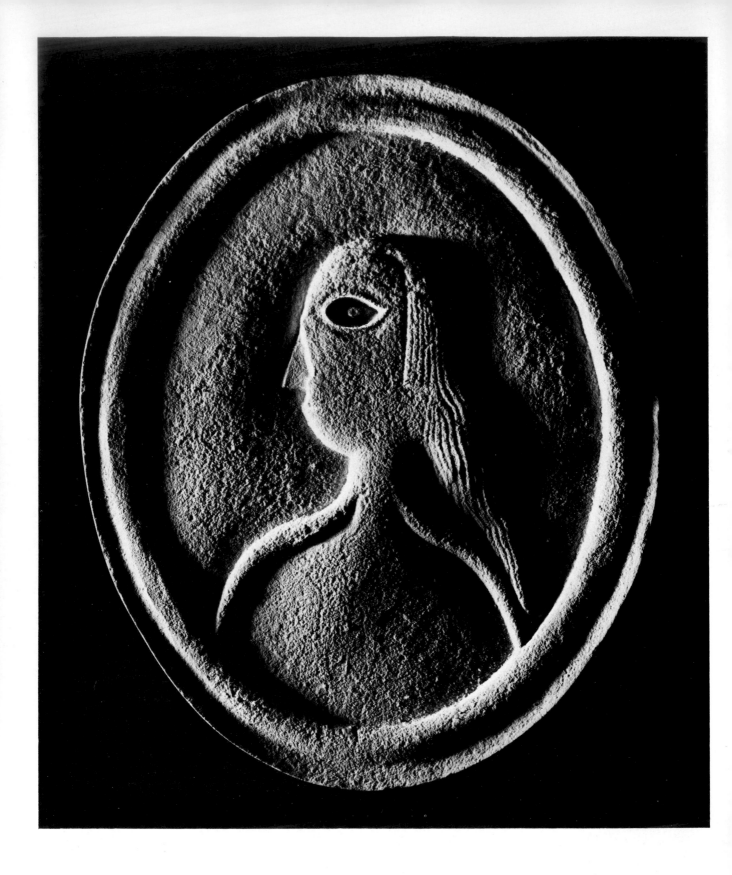

ABOVE: East Haddam, Connecticut, 1798. This slightly abstract portrait tops Amasa Brainard's brownstone. The inscription records that "he received a mortal wound on his head by the falling of a weight from the bell as he was about to enter the church to attend on divine worship." OPPOSITE TOP: Rockingham, Vermont, 1799. On this stone the Bellows youngsters are wearing nightcaps as they lie under their quilt. The epitaph, "sleep on sweet babes & take your rest, god cald you home he thought it best," reinforces the tympanum imagery. OPPOSITE BOTTOM: Rockingham, Vermont, 1799. This fanciful carving tops Margaret Campbell's slate memorial, which is probably from the Wright family workshop.

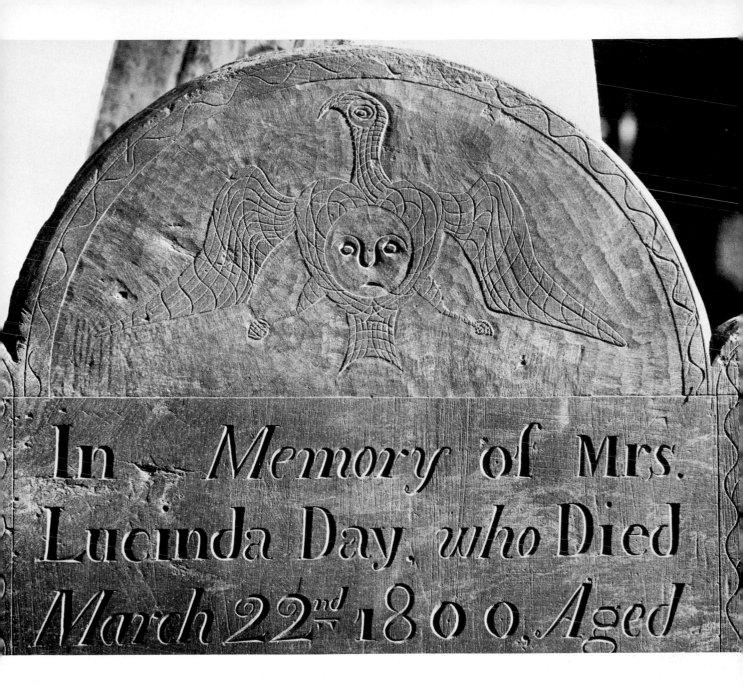

In Memory of Mrs. Lucinda Day, who Died March 22nd 1800, Aged

OPPOSITE TOP LEFT: Meriden, Connecticut, 1800. The Sarah Yale memorial displays the precise, geometric style favored by lower Connecticut River valley cutters. **OPPOSITE TOP RIGHT**: East Glastonbury, Connecticut, 1800. Young William Holmes's portrait stands out in high relief from the surface of the coffin-shaped brownstone memorial. **OPPOSITE BOTTOM**: Roxbury, Connecticut, 1800. The image of hands on New England gravestones may signify spiritual devotion. It appears on few memorials in western Connecticut and is invariably accompanied by a winged effigy. Only a very few of these stones also bear the heart symbol. **ABOVE**: Chester, Vermont, 1800. Lucinda Day's slate is famous for its symbolism, a soul orb being transported to heaven in the belly of an eagle. This design is attributed to the Wright family of carvers from southern Vermont.

OPPOSITE TOP: Chester, Vermont, 1800. The childlike quality of Stephens Riggs's slate tympanum is most unusual. Grieving figures stand at either side of a cinerary urn, while a heavenly trumpeter hovers above. The inscription records that "he was 16 feet, 2 ins, and was devoted to the navel service of his country." OPPOSITE BOTTOM: New York City, 1802. Elizabeth Guthrie died at the age of four.

On her small memorial in Trinity Churchyard she appears as a cherub, ascending to heaven and bidding farewell to earthly life. ABOVE: Peterborough, New Hampshire, 1802. For many years the main attraction at the East Hill Cemetery has been this carving of the angel Gabriel on Charles Stuart's large slate memorial.

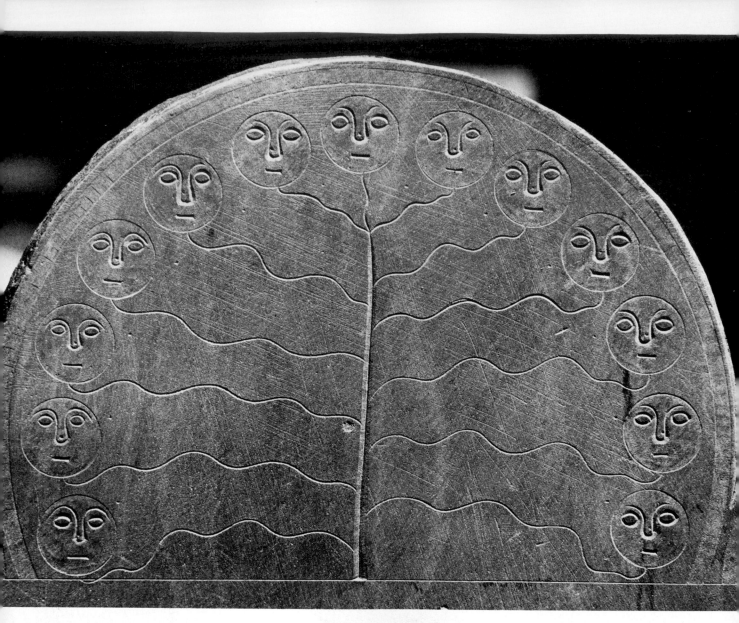

OPPOSITE TOP: Grafton, Vermont, 1803. The left tympanum of the Parks family memorial features the thirteen children, symbolized by soul orbs on a tree of life. This style is attributed to the Wright family, which showed great skill at linear slate carving. OPPOSITE BOTTOM LEFT: Portland, Maine, 1806. This superbly detailed slate coat of arms marks the grave of an infant. The epitaph reads: "Betwixt his birth & death HOW SHORT THE SPACE?" OPPOSITE BOTTOM RIGHT: Portsmouth, New Hampshire, 1808. A willow, a cloud and an angel decorating a tomb appear on this primitively carved slate. ABOVE: Wytheville, Virginia, 1805. Laurence Krone carved a symbol of the renewal of life at the ground line of Daniel Etter's gravestone.

ABOVE: Boston, Massachusetts, 1807. A century before this stone was carved, the figure of time was a common gravestone image. By the nineteenth century, however, its popularity had declined. This unusual nineteenth-century version of the time image appears on Henry Roby's slate in the Copp's Hill Burial Ground. OPPOSITE

TOP: Wilbraham, Massachusetts, 1807. The Hitchcock memorial unabashedly displays these two comical profiles. OPPOSITE BOTTOM: Wytheville, Virginia, 1814. This sun, symbolizing the resurrection, is attributed to Laurence Krone. It appears on the Jacob Repass memorial in St. John's Churchyard.

In memory of
Mr. Othniel and

OPPOSITE: Roanoke, Virginia, ca. 1810. To protect it from further vandalism, the "old tombstone" is now sheltered in a chain-link cage. The ornamental stone coffin displays the bust of a child; the removable lid was stolen some years ago. The sarcophagus tops a thick slab of sandstone resting on limestone blocks. It is inscribed in Latin, German and English and includes "A Famaly Rigester" of the Dentons, who commissioned it. One of its corners bears the name of Laurence Krone, the itinerant carver who left a trail of unusual memorials throughout southwestern Virginia. ABOVE: Crockett, Virginia, ca. 1820. This small gravestone from the Zion Churchyard is uninscribed. The meaning of its bold symbolism remains obscure.

OPPOSITE TOP: Wiscasset, Maine, 1814. Four images occupy the tympanum of Col. David Payson's slate memorial: a Masonic emblem, symbols of his military profession, an effigy (defaced by vandals) and a vine. OPPOSITE BOTTOM: Portsmouth, New Hampshire, 1815. This cherub, with an unusual wing design, is from the double-effigy slate memorial of the Hart family. ABOVE: Circleville, Ohio, 1825. Mary Taylor's sandstone memorial displays motifs representing the bounty of the afterlife alongside somewhat smaller mortality symbols. This early Ohio gravestone retains much of the symbolism common to eighteenth-century New England headstones.

In
memory of
CAPTAIN OLIVER HUNT
who died

OPPOSITE TOP LEFT: Rural Retreat, Virginia, ca. 1820. This simple, moving memorial for an infant stands in the Kimberlin Churchyard. OPPOSITE TOP RIGHT: Tolland, Connecticut, 1818. Capt. Oliver Hunt's stone features a well-preserved cinerary-urn carving in a style popular in sections of New England during the early nineteenth century. OPPOSITE BOTTOM: Worthington, Ohio, 1825.

Highly refined craftsmanship distinguishes the imagery of this central Ohio Masonic memorial. ABOVE: Hampton, Connecticut, 1832. This marble medallion with a symbol of the Holy Ghost, one of the finest nineteenth-century marble carvings in northeastern Connecticut, is in the North Burying Ground.

OPPOSITE TOP LEFT: Ceres, Virginia, ca. 1820. On this memorial images symbolic of life, the soul and the heavenly abode are represented in ascending order. OPPOSITE TOP RIGHT: Crockett, Virginia, ca. 1820. This anonymous memorial bears twin heart images above a symbol of renewed life. OPPOSITE BOTTOM LEFT: Ceres, Virginia, ca. 1820. The heart motif appears on many of the gravestones in the Sharon Churchyard. This detail bears a carving of a tree of hearts. OPPOSITE BOTTOM RIGHT: Wytheville, Virginia, ca. 1820. This symmetrical rose tree growing out of the symbolic source of life is but one of many splendid carvings on the backs of two-sided memorials in St. John's Churchyard. ABOVE: Logan, Ohio, 1832. Maria Smith's memorial presents this superb portrait, unfortunately marred by vandals. The styling of this unique sandstone monument suggests that this craftsman's conception of gravestone portraiture was strongly influenced by printed illustrations.

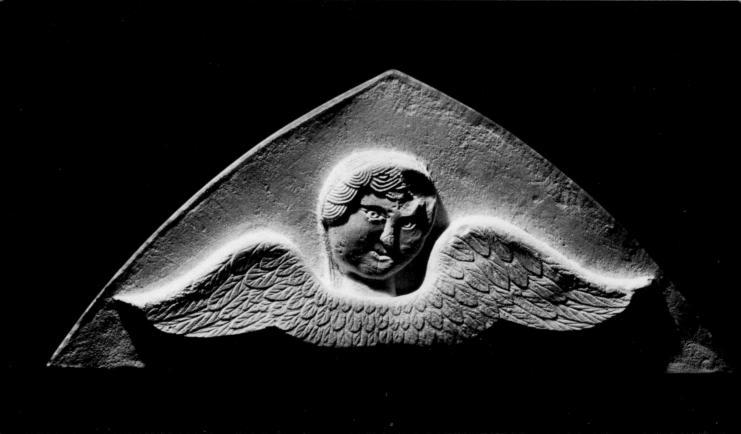

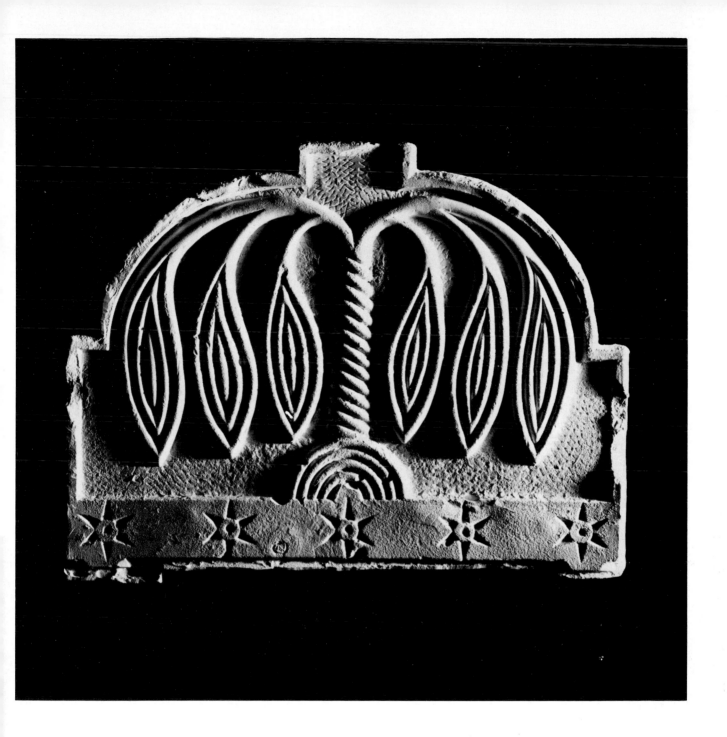

OPPOSITE TOP LEFT: Rural Retreat, Virginia, ca. 1820. This is one of many markers from the Kimberlin Churchyard that bear bold geometric designs. OPPOSITE TOP RIGHT: MacArthur, Ohio, 1834. This marble stone's imagery of twin doves in a willow tree is somewhat unusual as it is to the memory of a single individual. OPPOSITE BOTTOM: Granville, Ohio, 1833. This small effigy tops the monument of seven-year-old John Whipple, "who was killed by the fall of a tree" in 1824. Effigies seldom appear on Ohio gravestones; this is an example from an area settled by New Englanders in the early nineteenth century. ABOVE: South Bloomfield, Ohio, 1835. This style of willow carving found in a few central Ohio burial grounds, usually marks the grave of an early German settler.

ABOVE: Delaware, Ohio, 1837. The lamb and the willow were often united on nineteenth-century memorials, but rarely as touchingly as in this diminutive carving in memory of a child. OPPOSITE TOP: Delaware, Ohio, 1838. This neoclassical urn-and-willow motif was carved in local sandstone by an anonymous cutter of central Ohio.

OPPOSITE BOTTOM LEFT: Delaware, Ohio, 1840. Death and victory are symbolized in this willow-and-garland carving on Eliza Blanpied's sandstone memorial. OPPOSITE BOTTOM RIGHT: Amanda, Ohio, 1841. These elegant willow designs, lightly carved on sandstone, are infrequently found in Ohio's Lutheran churchyards.

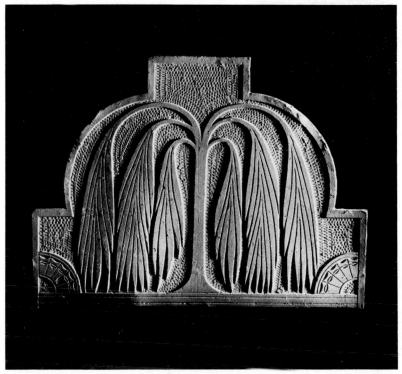

IN MEMORY OF
PENCY ORR,

OPPOSITE: Jacksontown, Ohio, 1837. Rebeccah Stanton's memorial presents a sculptural bust flanked by high-relief symbols of wisdom and knowledge. ABOVE: Liberty Township, Ohio, 1842. The Pency Orr memorial displays this unusual composition of nineteenth-century imagery by an unknown central Ohio carver.

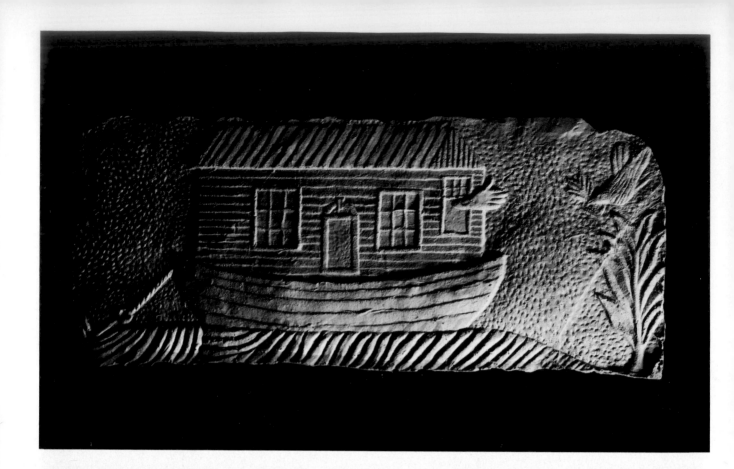

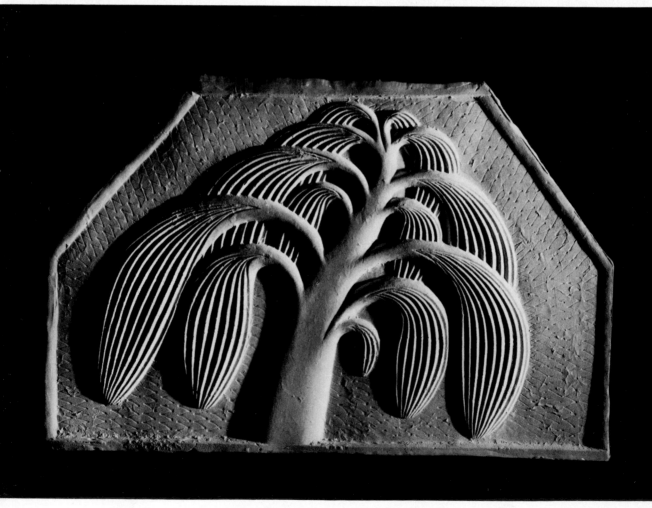

112

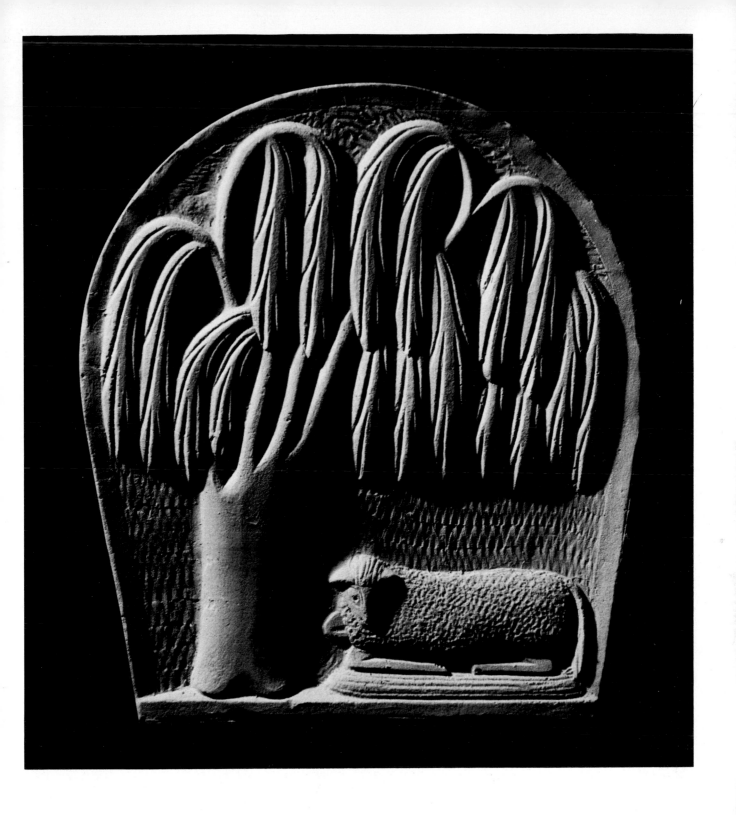

Opposite top: Stephentown, New York, 1843. The Benjamin Greenman marble memorial offers a rare carving of the symbolic ark of salvation. Opposite bottom: Washington Township, Ohio, 1847. This superb willow carving stands in a small roadside cemetery in Pickaway County. Above: Jefferson Township, Ohio, 1847. Lamb-and-willow motifs were usually reserved for children's memorials, but this example marks the grave of an adult.

In memory of
ELIZABETH
SPADE,

wife of
Jacob Spade who
departed this life

I rest in hope.

OPPOSITE: Washington Township, Ohio, 1845. Willow designs such as this one occasionally bear the signature of John Strickler, who carved many of the more striking memorials in central Ohio. ABOVE: Delaware, Ohio, 1849.

The mourning figure at the side of the grave appeared on many nineteenth-century tombstones. This carving from central Ohio is one of the finest from the pre-Civil-War period.

OPPOSITE TOP LEFT: Washington Township, Ohio, 1845. This formal willow design anticipates decorative styles adopted in the latter part of the century. OPPOSITE TOP RIGHT: Deep River, Connecticut, 1851. This front carving on a large marble obelisk is in memory of an enterprising seafarer. OPPOSITE BOTTOM: Gratiot, Ohio, 1846. Soul effigies are rarely found in Ohio burial grounds. This sandstone carving was signed by A. V. Smith, a talented cutter about whom little is known. ABOVE: Circleville, Ohio, 1861. This unusual marble memorial in the Forest Cemetery is a reminder that Frederick Van Heyde was a huntsman by profession.

OPPOSITE TOP: Bowmansville, Pennsylvania, 1850. This cherub medallion was carved in true nineteenth-century neoclassical style. OPPOSITE BOTTOM: Circleville, Ohio, 1862. This graceful rose carving is by A. Howard, a Columbus sculptor who executed several of central Ohio's finest nineteenth-century marble memorials. ABOVE: Brandywine Manor, Pennsylvania, 1865. On nineteenth-century memorials, the dove represented the purity and innocence of the deceased. This elegant marble is exceptionally expressive.

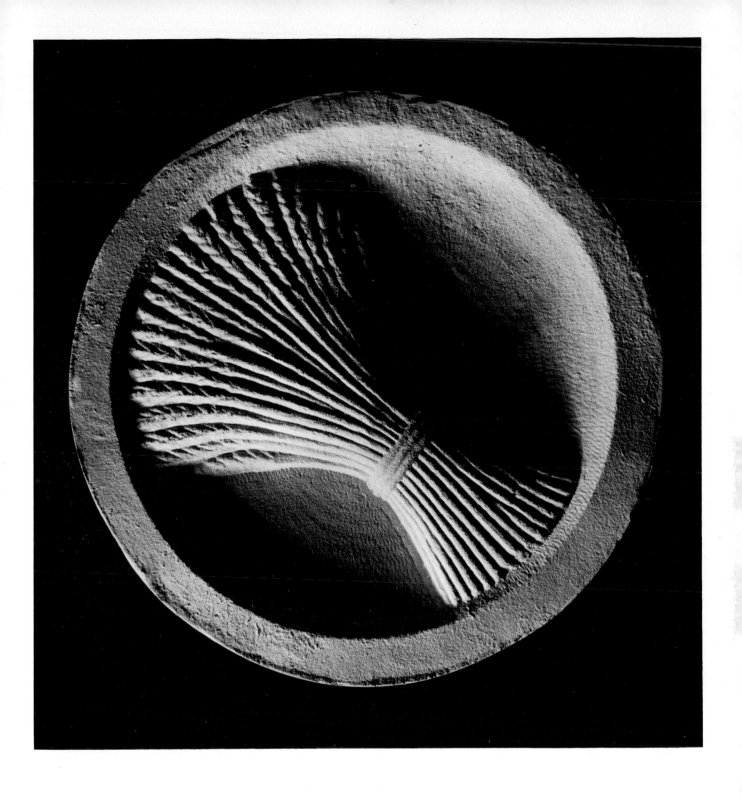

OPPOSITE: Lancaster, Ohio, 1855. It was considered proper during the nineteenth century to have one's profession depicted on memorials. John B. Reed's artistic occupation is made quite explicit in this marble carving signed by sculptor A. Howard. ABOVE: Jonesboro, Tennessee, 1872. The placidity of the Victorian era made the symbol of earthly harvest very popular on many marble memorials.

OPPOSITE TOP LEFT: Berlin Center, New York, 1864. A small hand points upward to a star on this infant's memorial, which is simply inscribed "Gone Home." OPPOSITE TOP RIGHT: Brownsville, Ohio, 1865. This Civil-War memorial honors a young Ohio guardsman who died "Of disease contracted in Southern Prisons." OPPO-SITE BOTTOM: Danbury, Connecticut, 1869. Austin Walbridge's lifelong association with the railroads is denoted by a profile of a locomotive on his marble memorial. ABOVE. Castine, Maine, 1878. The butterfly emerging from its cocoon represents spiritual purification and transformation in this marble carving from coastal Maine.

ABOVE: Woodstock, Ohio, 1895. This is one of the portraits modeled in concrete by Warren S. Cushman for the town's Civil-War memorial. OPPOSITE TOP: Bemis Heights, New York, 1887. Victorian sentimentality was expressed in "farewell" imagery, which became very popular in the latter part of the nineteenth century. OPPOSITE BOTTOM: Delaware, Ohio, 1903. Mr. Frederick P. Vergon requested that his favorite elm tree be shown on his slant-faced memorial in Oak Grove Cemetery. Sculptural in its relief, the large tree hosts cardinals, nests with eggs, an owl and a tree lizard, while bucolic scenes adorn the lower part of the monument. The memorial, measuring eight by ten feet, was carved out of one massive slab of limestone hauled from the Bedford, Indiana, quarries by M. V. Mitchell and Sons of Columbus, Ohio, contractors for the project.

124

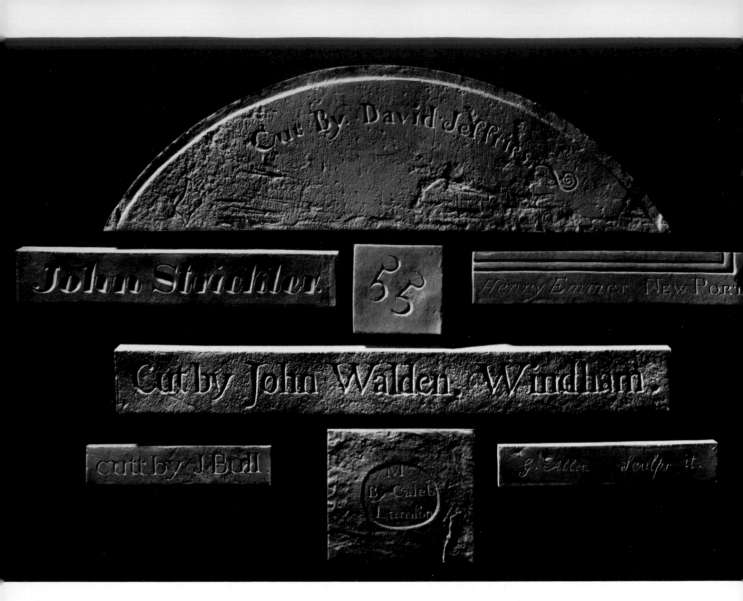

STONECUTTERS' SIGNATURES

1. "Cut By David Jeffries." Elizabeth, New Jersey, 1766. 2. "John Strickler." Logan, Ohio, 1845. 3. "55" (trademark). Milford, Connecticut, 1698, (a Boston area import). 4. "Henry Emmes, New Port." Barnstable, Massachusetts, 1763, (a Rhode Island Colony import). 5. "Cut by John Walden, Windham." Norwichtown, Connecticut, 1794. 6. "cutt by J Bull." Newport, Rhode Island, 1786. 7. "M By Caleb Lamson." Stratford, Connecticut, 1716, (a Charlestown, Massachusetts import). 8. "G. Allen Sculps it." Rumford, Rhode Island, 1799.

Colonial and American Stonecarvers of the Seventeenth, Eighteenth and Nineteenth Centuries

The great majority of gravestones were left unsigned, but diligent research can often disclose the names of specific carvers. If a regional gravestone style piques one's curiosity, one should start looking for specific carvers' names in the local town records. But first a few words of caution are in order. Individuals engaged in a variety of stone work were generally listed as "stone cutters," but only a fraction of these were in fact gravestone carvers. Only carvers specifically referred to as having been "paid for grave stones" can properly be labelled gravestone carvers. And even these carvers cannot be fully credited with the entire conception and execution of gravestones because relatives and/or apprentices often contributed to the projects. In general, attributions cannot be considered absolute even when the location, stone-type and date of the gravestone corroborate written records that the stone was purchased from a particular carver.

Dates inscribed on gravestones may also be misleading clues to the identities of carvers. Often, gravestones were cut (or inscribed) several years after the death itself. Such back-dated stones often replaced temporary or eroded markers. Others were erected on previously unmarked graves. (If, for example, at the time of the death, a family could not afford a stone, they might later order one to mark the gravesite.) Existing memorials might also be re-cut to commemorate more recent deaths: re-cut memorials were obviously less expensive than new ones. But these back-dated and post-dated stones present research problems: they may lead one to the wrong conclusions.

Pinpointing the correct town for research can be a problem in itself. The style of some carvers enjoyed wide distribution throughout the colonies. In these cases, the carver's home base must first be located. The sheer volume of stones in a particular style in one area makes such location easier. This kind of evidence does not, of course, help locate the homes of more nomadic carvers who left trails of memorials throughout the colonies. Some signed stones include the name of the town where the carver practiced his craft, but here again, such evidence is not conclusive. Signed gravestones are often found far from the carver's shop and were meant as a kind of advertisement for future commissions. A few enterprising carvers even incised the price of the stone near the ground line.

The tympanum-imagery remains paramount in identifying styles and carvers; nevertheless some researchers study border designs; others inspect footstones. There are, however, other ways of identifying gravestone carvers. A consistency (or even an inconsistency) in inscription carving, for example, often facilitates the identification of heretofore anonymous carvers. Here are some of the carving peculiarities that make identification easier: the prominence (or the lack) of incised guide lines, compass and tool marks; single or thick and thin chisel strokes in names, dates and epitaphs; the distinctive use of capital or lower-case characters (or the random mixing of both); punctuation marks (or the total lack of punctuation); backward characters and numerals (usually D's, L's, N's, S's, 4's and 7's); ligatures (connecting of characters); overscripts (smaller-size characters or numerals halfway above the main lines used either to camouflage bad spacing or for artistic effect); ungrammatical breaks in lines to accommodate runover of characters; frequent corrections (telltale over-carving or block obliteration of spelling mistakes, last-minute changes in ages and dates); abbreviation preferences ("Lt." or "Lieut." for "Lieutenant," for instance); the prevalence of the ampersand; distinctive formal introductory phrases (such as, "Here lieth . . .," "Here Lie the Remains of . . .," or "To the Memory of . . ."); the lingering use of "ye" for "the;" and phonetic spelling (such as "Margrat" for "Margaret" or "Febuwary" for "February"); and rarer others.

Gravestone attributions are always subject to revisions in light of further studies. The following information about the carvers reflects current data. The names of the carvers are grouped by state and each name is followed by the locality in or near which the carver was active. Birth and death dates, where available, are also included.

CONNECTICUT

Adams, Joseph. Killingly, active ca. 1790.
Baldwin, Michael. New Haven, 1719–1787.
Barker, Peter. Montville, active ca. 1760.
Bartlett, Gershom. East Hartford, 1723–1798.
Brainard, Isaac. Middletown, active ca. 1780.
Brewer, Daniel. Middletown, 1699–1763.
Buckland, Peter. East Hartford, 1738–1816.
Buckland, William, Jr. East Hartford, 1727–1795.
Buell, Benjamin. New London, active ca. 1760.
Chandler, Daniel. East Hartford, 1729–1790.
Chandler, Daniel, Jr. East Hartford, 1764–1853.
Collins, Benjamin. Lebanon, 1691–1759.
Collins, Julius. Lebanon, 1728–1758.
Collins, Zerubbabel. Lebanon, 1733–1797.
Cowles, Elisha. Meriden, 1750–1799.
Cowles, Seth. Kensington, 1766–1843.
Crosby, William. Chatham, 1764–1800.
Dolph, Charles. Saybrook, 1776–1815.
Drake, Ebenezer. Windsor, active ca. 1770.

Drake, Nathaniel, Jr. Windsor, active ca. 1765.
Drake, Silas. Windsor, active ca. 1765.
Gill, Ebenezer. Middletown, 1678–1751.
Gold, Thomas. New Haven, 1733–1800.
Griswold, George. Windsor, 1633–1704.
Griswold, Matthew. Lyme, ?–1698.
Griswold, Matthew, Jr. Lyme, 1653–1715.
Hamlin, John. Middletown, 1658–1733.
Hartshorn, John. Norwich, active ca. 1720.
Hartshorn, Samuel. Franklin, 1725–1784.
Hill, Asa. Farmington, 1719–1809.
Hill, Ithuel. Farmington, 1769–1821.
Hill, Phinehas. Harwinton, 1778–?
Hodgkins, Nathaniel. Hampton, 1761–1839.
Holmes, John. Woodstock, 1695–?
Huntington, Caleb. Norwich, 1749–1842.
Huntington, John. Lebanon, 1705–1777.
Isham, John. Middle Haddam, 1757–1834.
Johnson, Joseph. Middletown, 1698–?
Johnson, Thomas. Middletown, 1690–1761.
Johnson, Thomas, Jr. Cromwell, 1718–1774.
Johnson, Thomas. Middletown, 1750–1789.
Kimball, Chester. Lebanon, 1763–1824.
Kimball, Lebbeus. Pomfret, 1751–1832.
Kimball, Richard. Pomfret, 1722–1810.
Lamb, David. Norwich, 1724–1773.
Lamb, David, Jr. Norwich, 1750–1783.
Lathrop, Loring. Windsor, 1770–1847.
Lathrop, Thatcher. Windsor, 1734–1806.
Loomis, Amasa. Coventry, ?–1840.
Loomis, John. Coventry, 1745–1791.
Loomis, Jonathan. Coventry, 1722–1785.
Lyman, Abel. Middletown, 1749–1828.
Lyman, Noah. Durham, 1714–1756.
Manning, Frederick. Windham, 1758–1806.
Manning, Josiah. Windham, 1725–1806.
Manning, Rockwell. Norwich, 1760–1806.
Manning, Samuel. Norwichtown, active ca. 1760.
Miller, David. Middlefield, 1718–1789.
Ritter, Daniel. East Hartford, 1746–1828.
Ritter, David. East Hartford, active ca. 1810.
Ritter, John. East Hartford, 1750–?
Ritter, Thomas. East Hartford, ?–1770.
Roberts, Hosea. Middletown, 1768–1815.
Roberts, Jonathan. Killingly, active ca. 1765.
Roberts, Joseph. Putnam, active ca. 1765.
Spaulding, Stephen. Killingly, active ca. 1790.
Stanclift, James. Portland, 1634–1712.
Stanclift, James. Portland, 1692–1772.
Stanclift, James. Portland, 1712–1785.
Stanclift, William. Portland, 1687–1761.
Sweetland, Isaac. Hartford, active ca. 1800.
Tucker, Joseph. Bolton, 1745–1800.
Walden, John. Windham, 1732–1807.
Wheeler, Obadiah. Lebanon, 1673–?

MAINE

Dullen, C. Bath, active ca. 1830.
Emery, L. Bucksport, active ca. 1840.
Roberts, Jos. Portland, active ca. 1850.

MASSACHUSETTS

Allen, George. Rehoboth, ?–1774.
Allen, George, Jr. Rehoboth, 1743–?
Ashley, Solomon. Deerfield, 1754–1823.
Barber, Joseph. West Medway, 1731–1812.

Bentley, E. W. Lanesboro, active ca. 1840.
Bliss, Aaron. Longmeadow, active ca. 1840.
Codner, Abraham. Boston, ?–1750.
Codner, John. Boston, active ca. 1760.
Codner, William. Boston, 1709–1769.
Colburn, Paul. Sterling, 1761–1825.
Cushman, Noah. Middleboro, 1745–1818.
Cushman, William. Middleboro, 1720–1768.
Daugherty, S. Pittsfield, active ca. 1840.
Dwight, John. Shirley, 1740–1816.
Ely, John. East Springfield, 1735–?
Ely, John. Pittsfield, active ca. 1790.
Emmes, Henry. Boston, active ca. 1750.
Emmes, Joshua. Boston, 1719–1772.
Emmes, Nathaniel. Boston, 1690–1750.
Farrington, Daniel. Wrentham, 1733–1807.
Fisher, Jeremiah. Wrentham, active ca. 1765.
Fisher, Samuel. Wrentham, 1732–1816.
Fisher, Samuel, Jr. Wrentham, 1768–1815.
Foster, Hopestill. Dorchester, 1701–1773.
Foster, James. Dorchester, 1698–1763.
Foster, James. Dorchester, 1732–1771.
Fowle, Robert. Salem, active ca. 1765.
Fuller, Nathaniel. Plympton, 1687–1750.
Gaud, John. Boston, ?–1693.
Geyer, Henry Christian. Boston, active ca. 1775.
Geyer, John Just. Boston, active ca. 1790.
Gilchrist, James. Boston, 1687–1722.
Grant, William. Boston, 1694–1726.
Grice, Elias. Boston, ?–1684.
Hartshorn, John. Haverhill, 1650–1734.
Hartshorn, Jonathan. Newbury, active ca. 1755.
Hastings, Daniel. Newton, 1749–?
Hayward, Nathan. Bridgewater, 1720–1794.
Hinsdale, Samuel. Medfield, 1722–1787.
Holliman, John. Salem, 1704–?
Homer, John. Boston, 1727–?
Keep, George. Sheffield, active ca. 1835.
Lamson, Caleb. Charlestown, 1697–1767.
Lamson, David. Charlestown, active ca. 1780.
Lamson, John. Charlestown, 1732–1776.
Lamson, Joseph. Charlestown, 1656–1722.
Lamson, Joseph. Charlestown, 1731–1789.
Lamson, Joseph. Charlestown, 1760–1808.
Lamson, Nathaniel. Charlestown, 1693–1755.
Lane, Charles. Plymouth, active ca. 1800.
Leighton, Ezekiel. Rowley, 1657–1723.
Leighton, Jonathan. Rowley, 1715–?
Leighton, Richard. Rowley, 1686–1749.
Leonard, Barney. Middleboro, active ca. 1780.
Locke, John. Deerfield, 1752–1837.
Marble, John. Bradford, 1764–1844.
Marble, Joseph. Bradford, 1726–1805.
Marshall, John. Braintree, 1664–1732.
Maxey, Levi. Attleboro, active ca. 1800.
Metcalf, Savil. Bellingham, ?–1737.
Mulican, Joseph. Bradford, 1704–1768.
Mulican, Robert. Bradford, 1668–1741.
Mulican, Robert, Jr. Bradford, 1688–1756.
Mumford, William. Boston, 1641–1718.
Nash, Joseph. Hadley, 1664–1740.
New, James. Wrentham, 1692–1781.
New, James. Wrentham, 1751–1835.
New, John. Wrentham, 1722–?
Newell, Hermon. Longmeadow, 1774–1833.
Noyes, Paul. Newburyport, 1740–1810.
Park, John. Groton, 1745–1806.

Park, John. Groton, 1761–1811.
Park, Thomas. Groton, 1745–1806.
Park, William. Groton, 1705–1788.
Park, William. Groton, 1763–1795.
Park, William. Harvard, 1779–1854.
Phelps, Elijah. Lanesboro, 1761–1842.
Phelps, Nathaniel. Northampton, 1721–1789.
Pratt, Nathaniel. Abington, 1702–1779.
Pratt, Robert. Hanover, 1758–1830.
Savage, A. Lee, active ca. 1830.
Savery, Lemuel. Plymouth, active ca. 1775.
Sikes, E. Belchertown, active ca. 1790.
Soule, Asaph. Plympton, 1739–1823.
Soule, Beza. Middleboro, 1750–1835.
Soule, Coomer. Barre, 1747–1777.
Soule, Ebenezer. Plympton, 1711–1792.
Soule, Ebenezer, Jr. Plympton, 1737–1817.
Stebbins, Ezra. Longmeadow, 1760–1819.
Tainter, Benjamin. Newton, 1753–1844.
Tingley, Samuel. South Attleboro, 1689–1765.
Tingley, Samuel, Jr. South Attleboro, 1714–1784.
Tingley, Samuel. South Attleboro, 1752–1846.
Tinkham, Seth. Middleboro, 1703–1751.
Tomson, George. Middleboro, 1770–1845.
Tomson, Isaac. Middleboro, 1749–1819.
Tribbel, John. Plymouth, active ca. 1845.
Vinal, Jacob. Scituate, 1670–1736.
Vinal, Jacob, Jr. Scituate, 1700–1788.
Washburn, B. Kingston, 1762–1852.
Welch, Thomas. Charlestown, 1655–1703.
Whittemore, Joseph. Charlestown, 1667–1745.
Wilder, James. Lancaster, 1741–1794.
Winslow, Ebenezer. Berkley, ?–1824.
Winslow, Ebenezer. Uxbridge, 1772–1841.
Woods, Martin. Whately, active ca. 1795.
Worcester, Jonathan. Harvard, 1707–1754.
Worcester. Moses. Harvard, 1739–?
Young, William. Worcester, 1711–1795.

NEW HAMPSHIRE

Chandler, William. Lebanon, active ca. 1800.
Merrel, Peter. Salem, ?–1787.
Soule, Ivory. Hinsdale, 1760–1846.
Stewart, Jonas. Claremont, active ca. 1785.
Webster, Abel. Hollis, 1726–1801.
Webster, Stephen. Hollis, 1718–1798.
Wight, John. Londonderry, 1702–1777.

NEW JERSEY

Acken, J. Elizabeth, active ca. 1785.
Jeffries, David. Elizabeth, active ca. 1765.
Mooney, J. C. Union, active ca. 1810.
Osborn, Jonathan Hand. Scotch Plains, active ca. 1795.
Price, Ebenezer. Elizabeth, 1728–1788.

Schenck, (?). Springfield, active ca. 1800.
Stewart, Abner. Elizabeth, active ca. 1800.

NEW YORK

Zuricher, John. New York City, active ca. 1785.

OHIO

Cushman, Warren S. Woodstock, ?–1926.
Howard, A. Columbus, active ca. 1860.
Hughes, (?). Granville, active ca. 1850.
Hught, E. Hebron, active ca. 1850.
Humble, John. Cincinnati, active ca. 1840.
Ingersoll, W. S. Cincinnati, active ca. 1845.
Jeffries, W. P. Cincinnati, active ca. 1840.
Jungkurth, J. W. Lithopolis, active ca. 1840.
Meech, G. Lancaster, active ca. 1850.
Morten, J. A. Fulton, active ca. 1835.
Neely, N. Chillicothe, active ca. 1840.
Reeves, B. Fulton, active ca. 1850.
Smith, A. V. Gratiot, active ca. 1845.
Strickler, John. Logan, active ca. 1840.
Sutton, E. Jacksontown, active ca. 1840.
Walters, J. Chillicothe, active ca. 1840.
Wilson, G. Chillicothe, active ca. 1850.
Young, S. Chillicothe, active ca. 1840.

RHODE ISLAND

Angell, John Anthony. Providence, ?–1756.
Bull, John. Newport, 1734–1808.
Emmes, Henry. Newport, active ca. 1760.
Hartshorn, Stephen. Providence, 1737–?
Stevens, John. Newport, 1646–1736.
Stevens, John, II. Newport, 1702–1778.
Stevens, John, Jr. Newport, active ca. 1770.
Stevens, William. Newport, 1710–1794.

VERMONT

Adams, Joseph. Rockingham, active ca. 1785.
Adams, Sampson. Rockingham, active ca. 1785.
Baldwin, Asa. Dorset, active ca. 1795.
Booth, Roger. Bennington, ?–1849.
Clark, Enos. East Poultney, active ca. 1800.
Dwight, Samuel. Shaftsbury, active ca. 1795.
Dyer, Benjamin. Shaftsbury, 1778–1856.
Wright, Alpheus. Rockingham, active ca. 1820.
Wright, Moses. Rockingham, active ca. 1800.
Wright, Solomon, Jr. Rockingham, active ca. 1830.

VIRGINIA

Funk, Abraham. Rockingham County, active ca. 1825.
Hollister, W. R. Belpre, active ca. 1840.
Krone, Lawrence. Roanoke/Wytheville, active ca. 1810.

List of Select Burial Grounds

The cultural importance of colonial and early American gravestone art has been reaffirmed in recent years. Yet too many old burial grounds remain overgrown and abandoned, their art defaced, shattered and left to the elements. Each year, more stones vanish, the victims of erosion, vandalism and looting. But some communities have funded preservation programs to stem this onslaught. Concerned individuals have also volunteered time and effort to preserve the gravestone legacy in their local burial grounds. These steps have met with considerable success and they deserve to be emulated in other places where the local gravestone art appears destined to shameful extinction.

The following is a list of selected old burial grounds that offer much in terms of quality, quantity and history.

CONNECTICUT

New Haven: Grove Street Cemetery, Grove Street, across from Yale University (18th–19th c.).
Norwichtown: Old Norwich Town Cemetery, Old Cemetery Lane, near the Green (18th–19th c.).
Stratford: Union Cemetery, at the back of the Library (17th–19th c.).
Windsor: Palisado Cemetery, Palisado Avenue, in the historic section (17th–19th c.).
Woodstock: Woodstock Hill Cemetery, near the First Congregational Church, across from the Green (18th-19th c.).
Also Noteworthy: Brooklyn, Cheshire, Cromwell, Danbury, Durham, East Glastonbury, East Haddam, East Hartford, Glastonbury, Hampton, Lebanon, Litchfield, Mansfield Center, Meriden, Middletown, Milford, New London, Newtown, North Branford, North Guilford, Norwich, Old Lyme, Pomfret, Portland, Thompson, Tolland, Wallingford, Windham.

MAINE

Wiscasset: Ancient Cemetery, Federal Street, by the bay (18th–19th c.).
York: Old York Cemetery, Route 1A, near the Congregational Church (18th–19th c.).
Also Noteworthy: Blue Hill, Bucksport, Castine, Kittery Point, Machias, Portland, Readfield, South Windham, Vinalhaven, Waldoboro, Yarmouth.

MASSACHUSETTS

Boston: Copp's Hill Burying Ground, Hull Street, near the Old North Church (17th–19th c.); Granary Burying Ground, west side of Tremont Street, adjoining Park Street Church, near the Common (17th–18th c.); King's Chapel Burying Ground, east side of Tremont Street, north of the Granary Burying Ground (17th–18th c.).
Charlestown: Phipps Street Burying Ground, Phipps Street, at Lawrence Street (17th–19th c.).
Lexington: Old Burying Ground, near the First Parish Church, across from the Green (18th–19th c.).

Marblehead: Old Burial Hill, Orne Street, overlooking the harbor (17th–19th c.).
Northampton: Bridge Street Cemetery, Route 9, east of the town (18th–19th c.).
Plymouth: Burial Hill, Route 3A, behind the First Church and the Church of the Pilgrimage, at the center of town (17th–19th c.).
Also Noteworthy: Acton, Auburn, Barnstable, Belchertown, Billerica, Braintree, Bridgewater, Cambridge, Chelmsford, Concord, Duxbury, East Bridgewater, Falmouth, Grafton, Granby, Groveland, Hadley, Halifax, Harvard, Haverhill, Ipswich, Kingston, Longmeadow, Malden, Marshfield, Marston Mills, Medford, Middleboro, Milton, Newbury, Newburyport, Newton, Northboro, North Brookfield, Paxton, Pepperel, Quincy, Revere, Rowley, Rutland, Salem, Scituate, Sheffield, South Hadley, Taunton, Wakefield, Watertown, West Barnstable, West Newbury, Wilbraham, Woburn.

NEW JERSEY

Elizabeth: First Presbyterian Churchyard, North Broad Street, adjoining the church (18th–19th c.).
Also Noteworthy: Madison, Morristown, New Providence, Philipsburg, Springfield, Tennent, Union, Warrenville, Whippany.

NEW HAMPSHIRE

Claremont: West Claremont Burying Ground, Old Church Road, across from Union Church, adjoining the First Roman Catholic Church (18th–19th c.).
Hollis: Congregational Burial Yard, adjoining the Congregational Church, at the village center (18th–19th c.).
Also Noteworthy: Charlestown, Chesterfield, East Derry, Hinsdale, Jaffrey Center, Keene, Londonderry, Peterborough, Portsmouth, Seabrook Walpole, Windham.

NEW YORK

New York City: Trinity Churchyard, lower Broadway at Wall Street, Manhattan (17th–19th c.).
Also Noteworthy: Austerlitz, Bemis Heights, Easthampton, Harrison, Huntington, Kingston, Sag Harbor, Southampton, Southold, Stephentown, Tarrytown, Westhampton, White Creek.

OHIO

Delaware: Oak Grove Cemetery, Sandusky Street (19th c.).
Circleville: Forest Cemetery, North Court Street (19th c.).
Also Noteworthy: Brownsville, Cincinnati, Granville, Gratiot, Lancaster, Lebanon, Liberty Township, Logan, MacArthur, Washington Township, Woodstock, Worthington.

PENNSYLVANIA

Brickerville: Emanuel Lutheran Churchyard, Route 322, west of the town (18th–19th c.).

Ephrata: Bergstrasse Lutheran Churchyard, junction of Routes 322 and 222 (18th–19th c.).

Kreidersville: Zion's Stone Churchyard, Kreidersville Road, adjoining the church (18th–19th c.).

Also Noteworthy: Bally, Bern, Blainesport, Bowmansville, Brandywine Manor, Claysville, East Greenville, Hellertown, Huff's Church, Limerick, Mannheim, Muddy Creek, Stouchsburg, Stroudsburg, Williamsport.

RHODE ISLAND

Newport: Common Burying Ground, Farewell Street, first exit off the Newport Bridge (17th–19th c.).

Providence: North Burial Ground, North Main Street and Branch Avenue (18th–19th c.).

Also Noteworthy: Barrington, Bristol, Jamestown, Kingston, Little Compton, Warren.

VERMONT

Bennington: Old Cemetery, Route 9, adjoining the First Church, a mile west of the town (18th–19th c.).

Rockingham: Meetinghouse Cemetery, south side of Route 103, on the hill, adjoining the meetinghouse (18th–19th c.).

Shaftsbury Center: Old Baptist Meetinghouse yard, Route 7, adjoining the Meetinghouse (18th–19th c.).

Also Noteworthy: Arlington, Chelsea, Chester, Felchville, Grafton, Manchester, Sandgate, Sunderland, Westminster.

VIRGINIA

Ceres: Sharon Church Burial Yard, Route 42, adjoining the church (19th c.).

Wytheville: St. John's Lutheran Burial Yard, Route 21, adjoining the church (19th c.).

Also Noteworthy: Crockett, Fincastle, Roanoke, Rural Retreat, Waynesboro.

The Phipps Street Burial Ground, Charlestown, Massachusetts.

Alphabetical List of Gravestone Motifs

The artifacts left by past cultures enlighten the nature of the societies that wrought them. Early America's not-so-distant origin is especially revealed by symbolic gravestone carvings. These enduring witnesses attest to the early Puritan values and the subsequent interaction and evolution of religious attitudes, history, art and enterprise.

Anchors: The seafaring profession (18th–19th c.).
Angels: Heavenly hosts, guides (18th–19th c.).
Arches: Victory in death (18th–19th c.).
Ark of Noah (rare): Refuge, salvation (18th–19th c.).
Arrows: Mortality (17th–18th c.).
Bats (rare): The underworld (18th c.).
Bibles: Resurrection through the Scriptures, the clergy (18th–19th c.).
Books stacked (rare): Knowledge (19th c.).
Bouquets: Condolences, grief (19th c.).
Breasts: The divine, nourishing fluid of the soul (17th c.).
Buds: Renewal of life (18th c.).
Bugles: Resurrection, the military profession (18th–19th c.).
Candle being snuffed: Time, mortality (17th c.).
Chrysalis and butterfly (rare): Christian metamorphosis (19th c.).
Cinerary urns: Mortality, an occupied grave (19th c.).
Clocks (rare): Passage of time, mortality (18th c.).
Clouds: The divine abode (18th c.).
Coats of arms and crests: Lineage, status (17th–18th c.).
Coffins: Mortality (17th–18th c.).
Crossed swords: High-ranking military person (18th c.).
Crowned effigies: Personal reward of righteousness (18th c.).
Crowns (rare): Christian righteousness (18th c.).
Darts: Mortality (17th–18th c.).
Doves: The soul, purity (18th–19th c.).
Eagles (rare): The heavenly conveyor (18th–19th c.).
Eagles, as national emblem: The military professional, Civil-War casualties (19th c.).
Effigies: The soul (18th c.).
Father Time: Mortality, the grim reaper (17th c.).
Felled trees: Mortality (18th c.).
Field artillery (rare): The military profession (18th–19th c.).
Flowers: Brevity of earthly existence, sorrow (18th–19th c.).
Flying birds: The flight of the soul (18th–19th c.).
Fruits: Eternal plenty (17th–18th c.).
Garlands: Victory in death (18th–19th c.).
Gourds: The coming to be and passing away of all earthly matters (17th–18th c.).
Imps: Mortality, the uncertainty of afterlife (17th c.).
Hand of God chopping: Mortality, sudden death (18th c.).
Hand of God pointing upward: The way to the reward of the righteous (19th c.).
Hands (rare): Devotion, prayer (18th–19th c.).

Handshakes: Farewell to earthly existence (19th c.).
Hearts: The soul in bliss, the abode of the soul, love of Christ (18th–19th c.).
Hooped snake (rare): Eternity (18th–19th c.).
Horns: Resurrection (18th c.).
Hourglasses: Swiftness of time (17th–18th c.).
Lambs: Innocence (19th c.).
Lamps (rare): Eternal life (19th c.).
Muskets (rare): The military profession, a professional huntsman (18th–19th c.).
Orbs, as celestial bodies: The reward of the resurrection (18th–19th c.).
Orbs, as effigies: The soul (18th–19th c.).
Pallbearers: Mortality (17th–18th c.).
Palls: Mortality (17th–18th c.).
Palms (rare): Victory in death (18th–19th c.).
Peacocks (rare): Immortality, incorruptibility of the flesh (18th c.).
Picks and shovels: Mortality (17th c.).
Portals: Passageways to the eternal journey (17th–18th c.).
Portraits: Stylized likenesses of the deceased (18th–19th c.).
Roosters (rare): The awakening from the fall from grace, repentance (18th c.).
Rose offerings: Condolence, sorrow (19th c.).
Roses: The brevity of earthly existence (of English descent: the Tudor rose) (18th–19th c.).
Scythes: Time, the divine harvest (17th–18th c.).
Severed branch(es): Mortality (18th c.).
Sheaves of wheat: Time, the divine harvest (19th c.).
Shells: The pilgrimage of life, birth, life (18th–19th c.).
Ships' profiles: The seafaring profession (18th–19th c.).
Shrines (rare): Wisdom, knowledge (18th–19th c.).
Skeletons: Mortality (17th–18th c.).
Skulls and crossbones: Mortality (17th–18th c.).
Stations in life: A representation of the occupation of the deceased, sometimes in portrait form (18th–19th c.).
Suns: Resurrection (18th–19th c.).
Suns, moons and stars: The reward of the resurrection (18th–19th c.).
Swords: The military profession (17th–18th c.).
Thistles: Of Scottish descent: the inevitability of death, remembrance (18th c.).
Tombs: Mortality (18th–19th c.).
Torches upside-down (rare): Mortality (19th c.).
Trees: Life, the tree of life (18th c.).
Trumpeters: Heralds of the resurrection (18th c.).
Vines: Wine: the symbolic blood of Christ (18th c.).
Willows: Earthly sorrow, the symbolic tree of human sadness (19th c.).
Winged death's heads: Mortality (17th–18th c.).
Winged effigies: The soul, the flight of the soul (18th c.).
Winged hourglasses: The swift passage in earthly time (17th–18th c.).
Wreaths: Victory in death (18th–19th c.).

Bibliography

Barba, Preston A. *Pennsylvania German Tombstones: A Study in Folk Art.* Allentown, Pennsylvania: Schlecter's, 1954.

Benes, Peter. *The Masks of Orthodoxy: Folk Gravestone Carving in Plymouth County, Massachusetts, 1689–1805.* Amherst, Massachusetts: University of Massachusetts Press, 1977.

————. Monographs on various New England stonecarvers in *Old Time New England* 60: 13–30; 64: 30–41; in *Essex Institute Historical Collections* 109: 152–164; 111: 53–64; and in *Historical New Hampshire* 28: 221–240.

Benes, Peter, ed. *Puritan Gravestone Art: The Dublin Seminar for New England Folk Life Annual Proceedings, 1976.* Dublin, New Hampshire: Boston University and the Dublin Seminar for New England Folk Life, 1977.

Buckeye, Nancy. "Samuel Dwight: Stone Carver of Bennington County, Vermont." *Vermont History* 43: 208–216.

Caulfield, Ernest. Monographs on various Connecticut stone carvers in the *Bulletin of the Connecticut Historical Society* 16: 1–5; 16: 25–31; 17: 1–6; 18: 25–32; 19: 105–108; 21: 1–21; 23: 33–39; 25: 1–6; 27: 76–82; 28: 22–29.

Coffin, Margaret M. *Death in Early America: The History and Folklore of Customs and Superstitions of Early Medicine, Funerals, Burials and Mourning.* Nashville, Tennessee: Thomas Nelson, Inc., 1976.

Corrigan, David J. "Symbols and Carvers of New England Gravestones." *Journal of the New Haven Colony Historical Society* 24: 1–15.

Duval, Francis Y. and Ivan B. Rigby. "A Bicentennial Project." *Hasselblad* 1.1: 22–29.

————. "American Folk Art in Stone." *Print* 27.2: 62–67.

————. "American Gravestones: A Resurgence in Interest." *Idea* 21.121: 66–75.

————. "American Stonecutters' Art Exhibition." *Monumental News-Review* 87. 11: 10–13.

————. "Early American Gravestones: The Iconography of Mortality." *Lithopinion* 10.3: 48–63.

————. "Inscriptions of Our Past." *Visible Language* 7.2: 136–150.

————. "Silent Art of Our Past." *American Art Review* 3.6: 70–85.

Forbes, Harriette Merrifield. *Gravestones of Early New England and the Men Who Made Them, 1653–1800.* 1927. New York: Da Capo Press, 1967; Princeton, New Jersey: Pyne Press, 1975.

————. Various monographs on New England stonecarving in *Old Time New England* 16: 138–149; 17: 125–139; 19: 159–174.

Forman, Benno, M. "New Light on Early Grave Markers." *Essex Institute Historical Collections* 54: 127–129.

Gillon, Edmund Vincent, Jr. *Early New England Gravestone Rubbings.* New York: Dover Publications, Inc., 1966.

————. *Victorian Cemetery Art.* New York: Dover Publications, Inc., 1972.

Kull, Andrew. *New England Cemeteries: A Collector's Guide.* Brattleboro, Vermont: Stephen Greene Press, 1975.

Lie, Jessie, coordinator. *The Old South Hadley Burial Ground: A Conservation Project Supported by the South Hadley Bicentennial Committee.* South Hadley, Massachusetts: South Hadley Bicentennial Committee, 1977.

Ludwig, Allan I. *Graven Images: New England Stonecarving and Its Symbols, 1650–1815.* Middletown, Connecticut: Wesleyan University Press, 1966.

Miner, George L. "Types of Early New England Grave Stones." *Rhode Island Historical Society Collections* 12: 32–45.

Neal, Avon and Ann Parker. "Archaic Art of New England Gravestones." *Art in America* 51: 96–105.

————. "Sermons in Stone." *American Heritage* 21.5: 18–29.

Potter, Gail M. *Stories Behind the Stones.* Cranbury, New Jersey: A. S. Barnes and Co., Inc., 1969.

Sandrof, Ivan. "As I am now, so you must be." *American Heritage* 11.2: 38–43.

Slater, James A. and Ernest Caulfield. *The Colonial Gravestone Carvings of Obadiah Wheeler.* Worcester, Massachusetts: American Antiquarian Society, 1974.

Tashjian, Dickran and Ann Tashjian. *Memorials for Children of Change: The Art of Early New England Stonecarving.* Middletown, Connecticut: Wesleyan University Press, 1974.

Taylor, Erich. "The Slate Gravestones of New England." *Old Time New England* 15: 59–67.

Wasserman, Emily. *Gravestone Designs: Rubbings and Photographs from Early New York and New Jersey.* New York: Dover Publications, Inc., 1972.

Wust, Klaus. *Folk Art in Stone: Southwest Virginia.* Edinburg, Virginia: Shenandoah History, 1970.